Welcome to Wherever We Are

Welcome to Wherever We Are

~

*A Memoir of Family,
Caregiving, and Redemption*

DEBORAH J. COHAN

Rutgers University Press

New Brunswick, Camden, and Newark, New Jersey, and London

Library of Congress Cataloging-in-Publication Data

Names: Cohan, Deborah J., author.
Title: Welcome to wherever we are : a memoir of family, caregiving, and
redemption / Deborah J. Cohan.
Description: New Brunswick : Rutgers University Press, [2020]
Identifiers: LCCN 2019012950 | ISBN 9781978808928 (cloth : alk. paper) |
ISBN 9781978808959 (web pdf) | ISBN 9781978808942 (mobi)
Subjects: LCSH: Cohan, Deborah J. | Parent and adult child—United States.
| Adult child abuse victims—United States. | Fathers and daughters—United
States. | Adult children of aging parents—United States. | Aging parents—
Care—United States.
Classification: LCC HQ755.86 .C635 2020 | DDC 306.874—dc23
LC record available at https://lccn.loc.gov/2019012950

A British Cataloging-in-Publication record for this book is available
from the British Library.

A version of chapter 5 was originally published in *Life Writing* 11, no. 1 (February 2014): 127–136, https://doi.org/10.1080/14484528.2013.838736, in the special
issue *Writing the Father*. Reprinted with permission from Taylor & Francis.

A version of chapter 9 was previously published in *Letting Go: Feminist and
Social Justice Insight and Activism,* ed. Donna King and Catherine G. Valentine
(Nashville: Vanderbilt University Press, 2015), 81–90. Reprinted with permis-
sion from the publisher.

Naomi Shibab Nye, "Valentine for Ernest Mann," in *The Red Suitcase*
(Rochester: BOA Editions, 1994), 70. Reprinted with permission of the author,
January 24, 2019.

♾ The paper used in this publication meets the requirements of the American
National Standard for Information Sciences—Permanence of Paper for Printed
Library Materials, ANSI Z39.48-1992.

www.rutgersuniversitypress.org

Manufactured in the United States of America

For my father, James Cohan. With profound love and with the hope and belief that if you were still around, you'd actually get a kick out of being such a big character here. Oh how I wish you could read me now.

For my mother, Naomi Marks Cohan, for first enduring this as life and now living it out with me as story. For graciously accompanying me as I do it so publicly. For generously, lovingly cheering this—and me—on. For being able to bravely look back with me, to retrace our steps, to question, to laugh. For showing me since I was a very little girl what's involved and what's at stake in doing anything truly creative or artistic. For the friendship we finally got to make and for all the love.

For Michael, for leading me back to access my own ever-exploding heart. For the curiosity after our first date to ask to see my writing. For the beautiful response that then sparked the momentum to write this book into being, for the still daily morning emails, for being the best weekend a girl could ever ask for, for all the crazy laughter at everything and nothing, for the equanimity, for the music and rhythms you have added to my life, for being my muse and keeping me writing, for holding my heart. I love loving you.

Contents

Welcome to Wherever We Are

Introduction

When I first set out to write about my dad, I thought my book would only be filled with stories of his abuse, his rage, my own resulting rage and grief, and maybe even his grief as well. However, the writing process revealed other emotions—things that surprised me, disgusted me, delighted me, and saddened me. At moments, I was glad to be reminded of all the love I still feel for my father and reassured of his love for me. I have anguished over whether in my promise to tell about my father's abuse with integrity and honesty, the story would somehow be diminished by this other story of the great love we shared. It is only now that I see that the once seemingly pure story of his abuse is not even a pure story, and interestingly, I don't think the abuse is even the grittiest or rawest part of the story. As it turns out, the story would be easier to tell if all I needed to do was report about all the times my dad behaved badly. You might get angry with him and you might even feel sorry for me, but that's not what I wanted out of this book. You need to also know and feel the love we shared the way I felt it and still do.

The much harder story to tell is the one that unfolds in these pages. It's the story of ambivalence. Of what it means to stand on a precipice of both love and fear and what it means to navigate between forgiveness and blame, care and disregard, and resilience and despair.

I remember some years back that I shared my idea for this book with a colleague who works in film studies, and he said, "I can imagine if it were a film, the trailer would be something like, 'Caring for the parent who didn't care for us.'" It sure sounded like a great, slick line. Since then, over the years of describing this project to other people, they have summed it up much the same way as my colleague, attempting to package it neatly and absolutely, without much gray area. It is as though people were interpreting that there is care, and then there's the absence of care.

But the thing is, that rendering is less than truthful. This is indeed a story about what it means to provide caregiving for an abuser—in this case, my father. But it's also a story about trying to care well and lovingly for him in spite of—*and maybe even because of*—his history of abuse. Caregiving for an aging and ill parent is a common enough—though altogether gruesome—experience. And witnessing and experiencing family violence is also a painfully common reality. As a culture, it seems that we have slowly learned to be able to talk more about each phenomenon, thus removing some of the pain, isolation, stigma, and turmoil of each. Yet in my experience, nowhere do we really talk deeply about what happens when these experiences collide, then coexist and intertwine—in other words, what it means to care for an aging and ill parent who also happens to have been an abuser. So this book is about caregiving against the backdrop of these extremely complicated family dynamics.

Abuse and caregiving each demand a sense of loyalty and attention. Abusers, while behaving badly themselves, insist that we stand by on good behavior and acquiesce to their entitlement and destruction. The act of caregiving necessitates loyalty and asks us to pay attention. Part of the task of recovering and then writing this book has been untangling and reconciling these colliding and conflicting loyalties. By doing that, I've been able to access greater redemption for my father and for myself, hopefully positioning me to better offer some guidance and assurance to readers who are on these difficult paths.

I first set out to write this book for myself because my head was about to explode, and writing helps one go inward and then back outward. I did what I tell my students to do—to write so they can think more clearly, to write as a way to come to know. I also knew deep down that I needed to better reconcile for myself personally that which I lecture and teach about constantly—the multidimensionality of abusers and survivors and the sense of ambivalence that is so often present in cases of family violence.

I learned an awful lot about abusers' tactics and strategies while working in battering intervention programs. I started that work when I was twenty-four, quite a dauntingly formative time for thinking about intimate relationships, marriage, and family. As I spent countless nights in crowded rooms in subterranean spaces doing this work, I remember that I often thought to myself, "What happens to your world as a woman when you devote your life to helping men change?" That sobering and frightening question pushed the hardest at me when I came to see that the person whose behavior and attitudes I most cared to see change were my dad's, yet it seemed virtually impossible to make headway in that direction.

I soon realized I needed and wanted to write a story that might reduce other people's suffering. I knew that while neither caregiving nor abuse is unique, I was in a relatively unique position to start a conversation contemplating the complex nexus of the relationships of these experiences. As a sociologist interested in family violence and gender, I knew I had the capacity to see the following, among other things: how family secrets are maintained, how caregiving is gendered, and the myriad ways that individual issues we wrestle with in our private homes are actually connected to larger issues of the family as a social institution and to other social structures.

Family violence is a dynamic process, not an event, that unfolds and takes varying shapes and forms, often over years, and I have come to see how it can be lodged in caregiving. Caregiving, while also a process and not an event, can be lodged in a context of family violence.

For me, healing from family violence has been multi-pronged and has occurred in a variety of contexts. Besides therapy, which I think is profoundly useful, I have found healing through teaching and researching about family violence, counseling abusers, working with survivors, and writing about it academically. But far and away, the most significant healing has occurred for me in two ways: first, perhaps surprisingly, actually being nestled in the uncomfortable, painful, and intimate caregiving relationship with my father, and second, writing about that creatively in memoir. I never would have imagined that healing from abuse could have occurred in the context of caregiving, but for me, it did.

My dad was very sick for close to eight years, and this gave me time to reflect on and wrestle with the complexity of his behavior and personality and the effects these had on me. His was a long death, slow in coming, a death that seemed to never end as he got sicker and sicker but still lingered on. In this book, I reflect on those eight years as well as the five years after my parents split up, before he got so sick and when I was still enmeshed in other complicated ways of caring for him.

It was in the contexts of caregiving and writing that I have had to think about my resistance to my dad's abuse, his affection, his illnesses, and ultimately his death and also all the things that drew me close to him—to his abuse, his affection, his illnesses, and his death. Yes, precisely the same things that repelled me had a gravitational pull.

I remember, in one of the very first memoir workshops that I took in Boston, looking around the overly crowded seminar table and thinking, "Will there really be room for all our memoirs? Who will read them all? Does the world need so many stories of the same things?" And then an older Chinese woman said as we introduced ourselves, "My ears are overworked. My mouth is never used." Across the table, a Vietnamese woman said, "My life is not big enough to write." I wondered if perhaps they were revealing something about the Asian community, and by having the guts to be there, perhaps they were breaking a code of cultural silence.

I felt at once so different from these two women and yet so similar and did not know what to say. I sat there awed by what struck me as both the seamlessness and the cleavages between cultures. All I could think about was how my own life felt almost too big and too overwhelming to write about. Yet when looking at these women, who were much older than I was, were multilingual, and had lived in several countries, my life seemed small, narrow by comparison. And in the verbally chaotic home from which I came—Jewish, upper-middle class, verbally abusive, with a drippy degree of verbal and cultural capital—I was raised to believe that my voice mattered and was to be used, that words were powerful, and that my life, if lived well, had the potential to be larger than life. I grew up in a family in which the word was huge, in which it was wielded with great force, pride, terror, affection, vengeance, brilliance, creativity, and also intimacy. This is not to say that the Chinese and Vietnamese women's vantage points, fears, concerns, and censorship imposed by others and self-censorship were in any way completely foreign to me. The underlying sentiment they shared appeared to be this tenuous quality of women's voices, the precarious position of women's lives. And that surely resonated with me. Disregard of women was something I deeply understood and had devoted my life to change. Puncturing family secrets, breaking silences, and speaking out mattered in that early memoir workshop and still do.

I am a sociologist interested in qualitative research methods, and I am drawn to case studies for their energy, depth, vibrancy, and richness. In a case study, there's a total definitiveness, a no-holds-barred look at the subject at hand, yet there's also an inherent sense of partial truth and ambiguity. There are parallels between the case study and the memoir. In memoir, there's an all-consuming, obsessive examination of the specificity of one's experience dependent on how memory shapes and distorts us. It's like a life in fragments under the most intense microscope. It's the case study of our own lives.

In this book, I take readers to times and places that scared me, worried me, consumed me, and still do. While writing this memoir, I tried to be attentive to some of the central questions and debates in the field of family violence as well as questions I am often asked when I teach and give public talks. I approached the book this way because of the weighty responsibility I feel to write about this topic, to open up and share my life buttressed by the insights I have gleaned from the field and from teaching over the years.

Like many other sociologists, I operate from the assumption that good sociology has at its core an interest in social justice and social change, and I am motivated by reducing other human beings' suffering. As topics of inquiry, domestic violence and violence against women offer us the possibility to think about the nexus of relationships among social problems, personal healing and recovery, and social change. So ultimately, my deepest hope is that readers who find themselves in the throes of caregiving, abuse, or both will find something of value in these pages and will feel less alone.

I am motivated by a constellation of questions that propel this book. I have been long intrigued with notions of "home" and "place" and what even constitutes home. I have longed to understand why and how people come home to each other or don't and how relationships come together and break apart, how we form community, and how we are often alienated from each other. I am interested in what we hold onto, what we let go of, how we remember others, and ultimately how we're remembered. I am also interested in how people come to voice, how we create space for our newfound voices, and how we forge wholeness, especially in cases when voice emerges from trauma and brokenness.

There are some central lessons I attempt to convey when teaching about family violence that find their way onto these pages: abuse ruptures human connection; it breaks trust; it manifests in a variety of forms—physical, psychological, verbal, sexual, financial, and spiritual and through neglect. It involves power and control and a whopping sense of entitlement. One person is treated as being less valuable than the other, and their needs and desires and interests are rendered subordinate to the other. Abuse is about forcing someone to do something they don't want to do or preventing them from doing something they do want to do. It's not episodic; in fact, it's actually patterned—there's a sort of connective tissue that exists between what we wind up calling "episodes" of violence, and this is, in large part, what keeps the victim seduced into the pattern of violence. Violence is not natural or inevitable. It creates webs of fear for its victims. Abuse is about threats. It does not need to ever even happen to create fear and to exert a form of social control. The experience of being abused in one's home can feel like living in a homemade jail, and the experience of abuse is oppressive, as its aim is to restrict, flatten, immobilize, or trap the other person.

On the pages that follow, I take mundane, everyday objects, activities, or events that we rely on to live our lives or to make sense of things that happen to us, and I use these to reveal and unpack extraordinarily complicated and richly layered life issues. These chapters are meant to both stand by themselves and be fully anchored together. Since this is an unconventional memoir, you can even read the chapters out of order. You might think of each piece as a meditation; as such, they are intended to be different riffs on similar themes. Just as meditation involves returning our focus and attention to the present-moment awareness, so too I return here to similar themes again and again, practicing and working with what these overlapping issues have to teach me.

You will notice as you read this book that many conversations, email and voice mail messages, and letters are inordinately recounted with a level of detail that might on the face of it seem almost unbelievable. With the tools I have as a researcher, I carefully took field notes during my visits with my dad at the nursing home, and I took notes on phone calls I had with him and health care providers who worked with us. And for years, I also transcribed voice mails that he left for me, and I had always saved emails and cards and letters. I think I did all this documenting, saving, and recording for two reasons. First, I wanted to be sure to remember what was happening. I knew that the best way to make sense out of the crazy-making situations I found myself in was to write it down. There were so many outrageous, almost unbelievable things going on, and there were many moments I thought to myself, "Oh, there'll be no way to ever forget this one." Yet I know that the experience of trauma can alter memory. Second, I think I intuited that one day I would want to go beyond just chronicling it for myself and would want to eventually write about it, hoping the story might have relevance for others.

If you're anything like me as a reader, it can be a daunting task to keep track of who's who in terms of family relationships; to me, it can start to feel indecipherable. For better and for worse, this particular story has the tiniest cast of characters. I am an only child and was raised by my mother and father in Shaker Heights, a storied suburb outside of Cleveland, Ohio. We were an upper-middle-class family, Jewish identified but not affiliated or practicing. Both politically progressive and ahead of their time in so many ways, my parents were each artists in their own right—my mother, a most talented abstract artist and printmaker and exquisite educator, and my father, an advertising executive who was more like a magician with words. My parents were each married and divorced before their friends set them up on a blind date. In his first marriage, my father had two children whom I would never come to know except for the one time they visited in 1980. I don't know anything about those prior marriages or that son and daughter, yet thanks to what you can find on the internet, it appears we share some similar talents, aesthetics, and passions in addition to some genetic material. And because my parents were largely estranged from extended family, I never had real relationships with those relatives either. After graduating from high school, I left Cleveland and lived in Madison, Wisconsin, where I went to college, and then moved to Austin, Texas, for graduate school. At age twenty-four, I moved to Boston, Massachusetts, where I lived for eighteen years before I moved to my current home of South Carolina. A week after I moved to Boston, I met a boyfriend who nine years later became my husband and then my ex-husband and is now my dear friend and still feels like family to me. His name is Mark. We made a conscious decision to not have children. Four and a half months after moving to South Carolina, I fell in love with Mike, a guy I would love to clone just to make the world more fun and funny. Mike was married twice before and does not have children of his own. Due to our jobs, we live two hours apart, but we love the arrangement. The intense love we share together and the solitude we each get are both freeing. The point of all this is to say it's from these people that I've learned and lived out love and family, how it gets built, bent, broken, and built again.

Life forces us to sit with juxtaposition. Abuse and love. Fear and hope. Memory and blank space. Joy and grief. Connection and disconnection. This book is an attempt to make sense of these family fault lines, primarily through the prism of my relationship with my father, an extraordinarily complicated man.

As a very young girl, I liked to doodle on the wooden walls of the stairs that led to our basement. This didn't seem to bother my parents like you might expect, and they often even commented that it was cute and endearing. I wrote "Hi," and I drew pictures of tulips and daisies and the sun and wrote above them "Nice things by Debbie Cohan." As you will soon come to learn on the following pages, I witnessed and experienced mean, cruel things and much that was ugly, but somehow I also saw beauty and goodness and was sure to make that feeling indelible on those walls. Even at that tender age, I recognized that some things are worth writing down, letting others see and take notice. As an adult, I have been unusually committed to writing about some of the not-so-nice things—the grim stuff of life that is heavier, darker, and sadder. But I have also come to see that more than forty years ago, the little girl on the stairs had it right—both stories are here because both stories are true.

1

Phone Calls

Years ago, I attended a lecture given by the psychologist Carol Gilligan, and she said, "The thing about patriarchy is that it takes place in the midst of intimacy." I think the reverse is also true, that intimacy takes place in the midst of patriarchy. She went on to say, "The ability to tell our story is interrupted by trauma." *Patriarchy. Intimacy. Ability. Tell. Story. Trauma.* Trauma disrupts ability. Trauma shuffles, scrambles, and pulverizes story. Trauma dislocates, dislodges, and decimates voice. I think trauma also makes story and voice possible . . . eventually.

Driving back from Mount Pleasant one Monday morning after alternately lazing around with Mike on the beach, in bed, and on a hammock all weekend, something my childhood friend Erica said to me weeks earlier hit me like a ton of bricks. She and I had been on the phone talking about a writing conference I had attended where I felt that someone had very much misinterpreted my writing. Stunned, Erica said, "I can't believe she didn't get it; it's just about a girl who tried to do the right thing by her dad." And then smack in the middle of that commute back to Bluffton, it occurred to me that was exactly it: I still am a girl trying to do the right thing by my father, both in writing and in life. I am aware that writing about his terrible qualities possibly makes me look like a fool for still adoring and missing my father. But you must understand my dad's erratic meanness, which was all mixed up with his erratic kindness. The erratic nature of it all actually became predictable—predictable erraticness, erratic predictability.

The phone rings. My machine picks up.

"Hi, this is Deb. I can't come to the phone right now, but please leave a message, and I'll call you back as soon as I can. I look forward to connecting with you soon."

Beep.

"Hi, Deb, it's Dad. I hope . . . you're the best . . . I can't believe you . . . why did you . . . how could you . . . how dare you . . . you little shit . . . *Beep.*"

Play. Believe it. Rewind. Don't believe it.

Play again. Don't believe it. Rewind. Believe it.

Delete? Save?

Delete.

Some things can be deleted. Just often not the memory.

One night, long after my parents and I moved out of the house on Morley Road in Cleveland and I was living in Waltham, Massachusetts, I decided to call our old number, just to see who would answer. I dialed and got the recording that the number was disconnected. *Disconnected.* Well, yes, of course. Actually, the wires had been tangled for years. Crisscrossed. Fried. Burnt. People tripped over cords. Over discords. Who was even listening anymore?

Connected. Disconnected. *Dis/connected.*

My father was financially generous, but he was also financially controlling in ways that came with strings attached and left me feeling beholden to him. It was August 2000, almost a year after my parents split up, and I was working on my doctorate. He had offered to help me pay for health insurance, so one night we were on the phone figuring out the best arrangement, and I suggested he go to the bank and put the deposit in all at once, just to make things easier on him. He replied, "You'd make my life easier if you'd commit suicide." I was speechless. He went on to say, "Your mother is a slut. She ran off to fuck someone she has not seen in fifty years."

Yes, my mom had left my dad and immediately ran back into the arms of her first love, Allan, a guy she met at overnight camp when she was fourteen years old. At the time, I couldn't understand it either, and I—and everyone else—wondered if theirs was an affair that had simply lingered on for years. My mother has always claimed that it was not, that they truly reconnected in 1999 after Allan lost his wife to complications from chemotherapy and a mutual camp friend told him that my mother was soon to be single. And I remain moved by what my mom has said to me over the years—that Allan is the first man she ever really loved. So at sixty-four years old, when my mother moved in with Allan, she got to come full circle. There have been times I've wondered about the real sequence of things, but in reality, I've never really cared. I understand that monogamy is a tender social construct that is often hard to uphold, and I would have forgiven her if having an affair was part of the story. In fact, my dad's behavior was all too often so impossible that I questioned her loyalty and why she stayed; I never really understood them together. Now at forty-nine, I understand it better, through the prism of my own love for my dad, my own loyalty to him, even amid all that went on. And at the same time, their union made sense. When I was a child, it was my definition of family.

What was complicated—and remains so even now—was how I learned that my mother made such a huge life change, leaving Cleveland after being there all her life. Before my mother leveled with me that she had already up and moved to Cape Cod, Massachusetts, to be with Allan, I had already discovered it for myself. My parents' marriage was a second marriage for both of them, and they were each relatively familiar with the names of each other's old flames. Soon after my parents split up, I was in Cleveland to help my dad clear everything out of the family house, prepare for an estate sale and house sale, and get situated in his new apartment. It was then that he shared with me that he suspected that my mother had reunited with Allan and that he remembered that Allan lived somewhere in Massachusetts. My dad knew Allan's last name, knew he was a dentist, and thought he was possibly retired. They had all gotten together when I was a very little girl when Allan had come to Cleveland for some sort of dental conference. My father believed that Allan was always pining for my mom. I decided to call information for Allan's number to either hear what his voice sounded like or see if my mother would answer the phone. It was about 9:30 p.m.; she answered and sounded half asleep. I nervously hung up. I got my answer.

To this day, I have still never told her that I made that call all those years ago. Maybe this is odd given how often I talk to her now, calling her sometimes several times a day or hanging up and realizing I still have one more thing to tell her or ask her. And the act seems so juvenile looking back, like I was a teenage girl with a crush on someone calling only to hear a voice and then to hang up.

With my father, I was charged with dismantling our family home, and I participated in helping him make a new life. I felt far too front and center with him. However, with my mother, I felt relegated to the sidelines, forced to watch her gallop forward into a new life without much discussion about her choices. I really just wanted to know where my mother had gone and what was motivating her, woman to woman. It was as though her life and sense of future were hurtling along, and my father and I were crawling our way through a quicksand of a new configuration of family. As is true with many little girls, there were times growing up that I wanted my father all to myself. And now, as an adult woman, I had it and no longer wanted it. Not by any means.

I wasn't okay with my dad calling my mom a slut on the phone and told him so. He barked back, "Then what do you think she is? Look it up in the dictionary. Okay, she's a whore then." He added, "Anyway, your mom stopped fucking me almost thirteen years ago. She didn't fulfill her end of the bargain." I really couldn't believe what I was hearing—the sex, the lack of sex, my dad being the one telling me this, and his belief that because they were married, he was entitled to have sex on demand with her. That part was what didn't sit right with me. It still doesn't.

No one really wants to know about their parents' sex life—or that they even have sex—but what I also came to realize was that it's even worse to know they didn't. It's much lonelier and sadder. I started doing the math in my head. If my dad was right, then I was seventeen when they stopped having sex. This means they had not had sex since my senior year of high school. I see sex as a barometer of a relationship, just as I see hugging and kissing as ways to gauge a relationship—who is the hugger, the huggee, who is the one who breaks from the hug first, the one who holds on. I never saw my parents hug or kiss in a lingering, leisurely way.

When my parents divorced in 1999, Mark and I were on a sabbatical from each other; we didn't get back together until 2001, and then we married in 2003. So in 2000, he was involved with a new woman, and I was dating. I went on a date with a man named Ted who told me that his parents had been married for fifty years and that they went away on trips for six to eight weeks at a time. I recall that he characterized their marriage as "superb." I had never heard anyone regard their parents' marriage that way, and so I sat awestruck, wondering what the daily fibers of a superb marriage would even look like. More than anything, I remember thinking, "What would my own life look like and what would my outlook on marriage be like if I could claim *that* as my reality?" I also worried, "What will this person think of me if they get to know me long enough to hear me say that my own parents' marriage was so deeply flawed?" Apropos of nothing I had said, Ted went on to tell me, "My dad never raised his voice." I still remember thinking two things: (1) God, my own father is so opposite to that, and (2) why do we typically refer to men this way? No one says, "My mom never raised her voice." Why as a culture have we grown so accustomed to men raising their voices in public and in private? Why had I grown up groomed to expect that was just the way? The following day, I called my mom to tell her about the date, and when I shared the conversation that Ted and I had, she said, "That must've killed you."

The crazy part of my parents' situation was how much my father claimed to still be in love with my mother. Very close in time to my date with Ted, I was on the phone with my dad when he asked me if my mother was still madly in love with him. He also asked if she and Allan were really in love. And he asked if she was still wearing a certain plaid flannel nightgown she wore when they were married. I was extremely uncomfortable with the conversations he initiated with me. I finally told my dad that no, my mother wasn't in love with him anymore. I remember that he said, "Oh, well, okay then. I guess I'll have to figure out how to live without her." Later on, my dad sent me poetry that he had written, and he made sure to enclose a note indicating that these were poems written for my mother and not some random woman. Do I believe that my father loved my mother? Absolutely, without a doubt, yes. Do I believe she loved him? Yes, of course, absolutely. That remains the hardest part of dealing with their separation and divorce.

Throughout my childhood, my dad was like an inflatable character you put on your lawn during the holidays, very much larger than life. Watching him begin to navigate a life without my mother was heart wrenching. This man, whose influence I had once so blown up in my mind, flattened before my very eyes. I watched him yearning for a life he'd never have again but really never tended to well enough when it was his.

For almost thirteen years before he died, eight of which he was very sick, I found myself lodged in an uncomfortably intimate relationship with my father. I came to understand the idea of emotional incest, having too much responsibility for my dad while my mother often managed to look the other way. And granted, she and I somehow forged a deeper friendship in the years when I lived in Boston and she was on Cape Cod, much deeper than we were ever able to when my dad was in the middle, because his behavior drove a sizable wedge between us, and her reaction to that behavior—sometimes colluding, sometimes distancing, sometimes acquiescing, sometimes resisting, sometimes withholding—didn't always make her very likable to me.

But in my mind, my mom was still missing from this thing we had called family. She was living a whole new life in a whole new place, and this tiny family of three was fractured. It would have to be remade. With each parent, I was tasked with having to make half a triangle feel whole. Half a triangle just becomes a smaller triangle, so you might think it is still whole. And it is, sort of, but not really.

The experience of doing this with each parent made it so that the other one still felt eerily, confusingly both dead and there, all at the same time.

On the first night of Chanukah, when I was about nine years old, my parents sat me down at the dining room table to give me a diary. This was a pretty clever gift, since they were about to present me something big to write about. Then they shared with me some secrets of their past lives. I remember very clearly the preface to what they said, the perfunctory remarks that always characterize impending big news: "We love you very much, and what we're going to tell you won't change how we feel about you, and it won't change our family. We just think it's time we told you. We think you're old enough to know this now." They went on to tell me that they had each been married before and that my dad had two children from his first marriage. In that moment, all that seemed to bother me was that I might no longer be able to honestly identify as an only child, something that was rather unique in the late seventies. I felt special, and when teachers asked how many brothers and sisters everyone had, I precociously corrected them and said, "But the question really should be, 'Do you have any brothers and sisters?'"

When my parents finally shared their news with me, it sounded like they had rehearsed it about nine hundred times. I guess we all do that when we have something potentially startling to share. We go to tell bad news or news that we know the other person will find surprising, and we become apprehensive. We rehearse the initial opening, the part we can control before we get their response. We review our intent. We rehearse it until our intent matches what we decide we want the other person to grasp, to understand, to feel. Intentions, effects, they all blur together, for both the deliverer of the news and the person receiving it. At that first performance of those words, the remarks often come out sounding clean, clear, polished, rehearsed, and understandable. And the person delivering the news sighs in that flat "Oh my god, I just told you that" sort of way. It's as if a firecracker explodes into the night sky, and suddenly there's a rush of light and sound, a pop and boom, a whooshing noise, and then a fizzling sound. What my parents never knew when they told me the news that evening of Chanukah was how that forever altered my understanding of family, of relationships, of marriage, and of my own place in our family.

On September 27, 1999, I was standing at the doorway between my bedroom and bathroom in a sports bra and leggings, having just come from the gym, and was about to get in the shower to meet a friend for dinner. The phone rang, and it was my mom. She said she needed to get my dad on the phone also. That was already odd, since I always had separate conversations with them and even tried to talk with them when the other was not around. The conversation we had was eerie; they began repeating virtually the same prefatory remarks they had said twenty years earlier, that first night of Chanukah. "Nothing will really change in your life. We're still your parents, and we both love you very much." And then came the popping, booming noise, more like a shotgun through a family than a fireworks display this time, and they told me they would be divorcing. So while they were careful to say that it would not change my life in any way, of course, this would become the furthest thing from the truth. I suppose that it would seem reasonable to assume that my life wouldn't change, since I was just about to turn thirty, my dad was about to be seventy-two just two days later, and my mom was turning sixty-five that winter, and they were each able to live independently and care for themselves. It's not like I was going to be shuttling between houses and trading off weekends and holidays with each of them. What I was about to learn, though, was how differently hard it would be to experience parental divorce as an adult child.

In mid-October 1999, I caught my first glimpse of what it would actually feel like to have to reconfigure our family's form. The three of us had been invited to the wedding of an old family friend in New York City, a place we had gone almost yearly to take in anything new offered in the theaters and museums. This time, my parents decided that they weren't ready to tell anyone about the divorce, that we would all just go on this trip and somehow fake it. This would be my last time seeing my parents married, together, on a vacation. It seemed preposterous to me that we had to hide something so funda-mental from dear friends. Predictably, family friends confided in me later, "How well did I know your parents if they did not share the real stuff of their lives?" and "Your mom was like the only one clothed in one of those open women's dressing rooms where everyone gets naked together and tries on clothes."

The night before the wedding in New York, I went back to my room and tried to fall asleep. Rather than count sheep, I counted family members. I had five family members. Just five blood-related family members I knew. One was shriv-eled up and dying in a nursing home in Cleveland: my grandmother; two were divorcing: my parents; one was sick: my aunt, my mom's sister, the one she had not spoken to in decades who lived in New York; and my cousin, also in New York, a highly talented fuck-up who was strung out in a mental hospital. The mental hospital was better than jail, where he had been for some of my childhood for holding up a doctor so he could get drugs. But I could really only speak with three of these five people anyway, since I was not in touch with my cousin, and Alzheimer's was rendering my grandmother incommunicative. I had this image of all of us lying in these very high buildings on beds of isolation floating aimlessly in the sky.

About a year and a half after my parents divorced, they decided to try to make a go of it one more time. My mom left Allan and moved back in with my father. It lasted a little more than a month, and she was right back with Allan. They all resembled fickle, giddy, defiant, and downtrodden seventeen-year-olds. Just before this, as it was appearing that our lives were spinning and crashing around in a sort of pinball machine of my parents' own making, my dad called me while he was drunk and left a voice mail on my machine, letting me know all about a lavish present he had purchased for my mom. I couldn't believe how disturbingly discombobulated his message sounded, but after all, he was obviously very drunk. This is what he said: "You are beautiful. You are phenomenal. You are getting smart. You have to move a little faster to make your PhD so you can get out and earn a living and be happy as a flea. I did that as I did it. And I hope you like it, and I hope you take it to heart. It is time to get off your *toches* [Yiddish for buttocks] and work for your PhD. Right, Doodles? Now, did you get anything from Mom? I think I sent you a clipping, and I think I sent Mom something, I don't remember, and a piece of jewelry for her birthday, which I think and hope she will love. It wasn't really jewelry. It's like a beautiful hammered bowl by John Hardy, who's supposed to be phenomenal. You can tell Mom that they are totally refundable at TJ Maxx. No, not TJ Maxx, at Neiman Marcus. It's extremely expensive, and I wish she would keep it, or if she doesn't keep it, I wish she would buy something absolutely stunningly beautiful with it [the money from returning the gift] because she deserves it. She's the best, and I love her more than I love myself. And I would gladly destroy myself to save her. She makes life worth living. She makes life. . . ."

And then, thankfully, the machine hung up on him.

I waited until the following morning to contact him and left a message asking him if he remembered calling me. I indicated my concern that his message sounded confused and that he sounded drunk. Well, to me he sounded pathetic, but I said drunk. Later that day, I got another voice mail from him: "I wanted to call you on your home phone as opposed to talking to you on your cell phone. I find it hard to buy your deep concern. When I called you last night, you said that was around midnight, and you waited nearly twelve hours to call me back. So your concern doesn't make much sense. So spare me your concern, Deb. And I just wanted to ask you another question—did you ever do anything on, let's say, a Tuesday, and someone asked you about it on a Wednesday, and you didn't remember that you did it? Does that happen to you? Because it's happened to me all my life, and I can't believe that I've been mentally sick all my life, okay? Deb, don't try to do this to me. I know that you have your problems with me and the way I feel about Mom, and that's just too fucking bad, but that's the way I feel, and I'm not gonna stop because it upsets you or makes you uncomfortable. Okay, honey? Just stay out of my business. Goodbye."

The very next morning, my dad called and left me this message: "Hi, Deb. Now, as far as this whole business is concerned with my alleged memory loss, I saw a neurologist this morning, and I'm going back to the Cleveland Clinic to see him again this afternoon, as well as the psychologist, and as well as the gerontologist. But the initial reports are that there is absolutely nothing wrong with my memory. The doctor believes that on the basis of some tests he gave me this morning, I'm in the top two percent of my age bracket in perception recall, about six other things, and he thinks that the notion that I'm losing my memory or my mind is absolutely absurd. He says I'm as sharp as any seventy-three-year-old person he has known and in fact sharper than many even ten to fifteen years younger than I am."

Beep.

Within seconds, he called right back: "So to finish, he's going to do some more tests this afternoon with the psychologist and the gerontologist. He did a blood test and a urine test and all kinds of things, and he said there's nothing to support the theory that I have lost any of my mental or memory capabilities. He does say that with the pain pill I'm on, that can cause the symptom of forgetting things, but it's not a forgetting where you forget it permanently. When you're reminded of it, it's recalled. However, he asked me not to continue taking it. And I got a steroid shot in my shoulder, and it's much better. So there's no need to take the medicine. So much for your theories, Deb. I wish you would stay out of my medical affairs. Thank you very much. That doesn't mean that I don't love you. I just don't want you involved in my affairs. Thanks, baby. Goodbye."

And then he called again. "Two more things, Doodles. Do you know anyone who has a clean bill of mental health from what amounts to three doctors? Ha ha ha ha. And number two: if you have spread this vicious information about me to anyone, I would appreciate it if you would straighten them out and tell them the whole story, which you now know. Goodbye."

A little more than fourteen months after my dad fell and broke his hip on ice at Cleveland Hopkins International Airport, he fell and broke that same hip again on his bathroom floor in the middle of the night. He had decided to try to walk on his own, unassisted, and it resulted in a horrible fall. These were the years when LifeCall phoned me constantly. People joke about that service, advertised on television with a commercial in which a fallen senior citizen presses a button to alert a LifeCall customer service rep that she's in trouble and signals that by saying, "Help! I've fallen, and I can't get up." But trust me, it's anything but funny when you are the contact on their phone roster. In late spring, my father was still in rehab at the nursing home from his fall, and I went out to visit him again and stayed at his apartment. He was certain he would get to return to his home—and he desperately wanted to—though it seemed increasingly impossible to expect this could ever realistically happen.

During the visit, I was bombarded with stacks and stacks of his unopened mail and bills. So much business had not been attended to. My dad had been someone who valued paying bills on time, filed everything, and was relentless about following up, even with annoying bureaucracies. So I knew he had really started to lose a grip on his ability to deal with daily life. The next day, I stopped to buy two extra large coffees and took them to the nursing home, where he and I sat in the common area and went through every piece of mail, and I helped him pay every bill. His money was quickly depleted. Within less than three months, it became clear that he had to give up the apartment, his car, his credit cards, everything. And then the phone calls and mail started pouring in from collection agencies wanting his money. When they couldn't get through to him, they called and harassed me, and they did this for years.

Calls to and from the nursing home quickly became maddening. Nursing homes will call the person who is named power of attorney for everything, and I really do mean everything, at all hours of the day and night. They have to for legal reasons. And there are no boundaries in nursing homes. I'll never forget the voice mail that said, "We're just calling because we found an open wound on your dad's scrotum, so we'll use some ointment on it."

Another time, I was leaving a movie theater and got a voice mail message that my dad fell out of his wheelchair onto a pad on the floor, and two aides were needed to lift him up because he was like dead weight. But they realized they couldn't do it, so they had to call an ambulance for help. I was constantly called, jolted out of whatever reality or joy I had gotten to construct for myself at the time.

Another day, while we were on the phone, my dad tried to convey to me that all the workers at the nursing home were doing a big presentation but were waiting for me to get my PhD so I could do some work with them. That might have been one of our saddest, most confusing phone calls. Obviously, there was no presentation. And my father, who for years wanted a PhD for me more than I sometimes even wanted it myself, had now forgotten I had already earned it a few years earlier.

Similarly, he was excited to know that I taught for a few years at Harvard and then a year later forgot that I ever did. He then asked if I was still teaching at the University of Connecticut or the Connecticut College for Women. I told him it was no longer called Connecticut College for Women and was simply Connecticut College. He said, "Well, who cares anyway. The name should really be Connecticut College for Broads."

When my dad stopped leaving messages on my answering machine, I knew he was slipping further away from me. I didn't want the hate-filled, accusatory, or crazy messages with which I was too familiar, but I wanted to know that as long as my dad lived in the world, he could reach out to me, could call me.

At some point, though, it started to seem like a waste for him to have a phone line in his room. After all, I was really the only one he spoke to most of the time, and as it was, he had trouble correctly making calls or finding the phone to answer it. One day, the nursing home called me to tell me that he had called 911 because he had lost twenty-two dollars. I really didn't know whether to laugh or cry. I mean, that is pretty funny, right? Think about the cops coming out to the nursing home because of a measly twenty-two dollars. It's pretty hysterical—and pretty fucking tragic.

I was less prepared for what would happen once I arranged for his direct line to be disconnected. Suddenly, there were many steps involved in calling my dad. I had to first call the main switchboard and ask to be connected to his floor and then had to ask the nurse or aide who answered the phone at the desk if she could go to his room with the cordless phone or could wheel him from one of the common areas to the desk to take the call. I think it was easier for them to tell me he was sleeping or eating, just so they wouldn't have to be bothered. When I was placed on hold, I heard wailing and screaming coming from other residents. Too many times, I heard the disturbing sound of a scared, weak man yelling, "Help!" It turns out that man was my father. Eventually, they brought him to the phone.

To this day, I can still hear echoes of that cry for help reverberating in my mind even though my father is dead. Anything—or nothing—could precipitate his cries for help. When I visited him, I saw that upon waking up from a nap, he would immediately yell for help just as he opened his eyes. It was as though all the help he had ever needed or wanted and yet never pursued was contained in those high-pitched cries toward the end of his life.

The nursing home: Paved driveway. Automatic doors. Cigarette butts. Patients waiting for the next distribution of cigarettes. Orange sherbet and ginger ale and Salisbury steak. Sticky floors. Dusty rose vinyl recliners. Bedpans. Bingo and sing-alongs. Stashes of adult diapers in the closets and drawers. Motorized wheelchairs. Schedules. Forms. Nursing aides and personal attendants. Styrofoam cups. Stale urine. Plastic water pitchers and bendable straws. Hospital beds. Dark, dingy rooms. A small rod for hanging clothes. Nonskid socks. No privacy. Open, unlocked rooms filled with demented wanderers. Whiteboards with washable markers stating the day of the week and the nurse on duty. Dead plants. Almost-dead people. Harsh overhead lighting in overheated rooms. Not enough real light. Tables that roll across beds for getting fed. Call bells and strings to pull in the bathroom. Air that doesn't move.

In one of the first nursing homes where my dad lived, the one where they distinctly preferred the docile, passive, little old Jewish ladies named Ethel, Gertrude, Ruth, and Frieda, they called to tell me that the cops had come for my dad. He had been throwing phones and water pitchers and called the staff bitches and whores. The nurse told me, "We tried to reason with him, to redirect him, and we told him you wouldn't call your daughter or wife that." "Oh, bullshit," I thought. "You really don't know my dad." They went on to tell me that he punched one of the aides in the jaw when she was kneeling down beside him, helping him move his legs. I was stunned. I immediately leaped into advocacy mode and recited what I was used to asking survivors of violence or abusers in groups.

"I am so very sorry. Did she sustain any injuries? Did she need to go to the emergency room?" I was told she was okay. I was momentarily relieved. Then they said my father was being sent to South Pointe Hospital to be evaluated. I swear, in the end, they may as well have had a shuttle bus for all the times he was taken back and forth, admitted, evaluated, readmitted, and reevaluated. A day later, when I had a chance to talk with my dad over the phone, I gently asked him why this had happened, why he had punched the aide. He tried to tell me, "Honey, the nurses said to me, 'Your daughter is a whore who sucks lots of cocks.' I had to defend you, Deb. I had to let them know that's not true."

In February 2011, a year and a half before my dad died, I went on a couple of job interviews, one in Upstate New York and another in Virginia. I called to tell my dad all about the trips, eager to try to share the details of my life while still unsure and uneasy about what he could actually retain and understand. He responded by saying he had just gotten back from Hawaii, from seeing gorgeous, exotic flowers there. There was no point in telling him otherwise. If beauty could be even a figment of his imagination in that godforsaken nursing home, let him have it, I thought.

My dear friend, Livia, who is more like a big sister, had astutely pointed out that the academic job market resembled military postings, with people being deployed and stationed in places they would prefer not to live. And with the belabored nature of the academic interview process wearing thin on me, I daydreamed about moving to a bungalow on one of the more remote Hawaiian Islands myself. It was oddly comforting that he and I longed for the same thing.

In those final years, I still called my dad to share the latest developments in my life, but he had less and less to share, and then nothing to share. I remember asking him, "What's new?" and I realize now that had to be the stupidest question to ask.

"I don't have much to say. I'm wheelchair bound."

"Dad, I'm so sorry. I wish there was more I could do."

"Honey, it's just a terrible way to end a life."

"I know." But, really, I didn't know anything. Nothing.

Other times, I would call my dad, and after telling him whatever the news was about my day, he'd say, "Deb, you wanna hear about me?"

"Of course, Dad, tell me anything you want."

"Well, my butt is killing me." And that's what our calls came to; that's what he had left to share. He was no longer alive in the real sense of that word. But he was alive enough for me to be able to be aware that I had a father, to say I had a father, to be able to call him, to be able to send him a card with an address right here on this Earth.

Time seems to move exponentially slower in a nursing home. I remember visits where I would arrive at noon and look at my watch thinking I had been there for two or three hours and only forty minutes had passed. I couldn't bear to stay, couldn't wait to get out of there, and yet was distraught about leaving. One of the hardest parts about having a parent in a nursing home is that their world is continually shrinking, rapidly so—even as time is slowed.

Close to eight years of my dad being physically sick, mentally unhinged, and in nursing homes brought with them a rhythm for how to negotiate his pain, his decline, and the bureaucracy and institution of the nursing home, and so I wound up learning a chronology of care. It went like this: he's sick; he's getting sicker; there will be an impending crisis, but we'll rally, we'll get resilient again; he will miraculously get a little better; we will get sleep, we will know hope; there will be moments that don't feel so heavy, and then boom, crash, more bad news, worse than the last time, so that we are left saying, "Wow, we thought he was so bad before, but he's *so* much worse now." Mark and I would say in disbelief to each other, "We didn't know how good it was when he could . . . ," whatever the "when" or whatever the "could" actually involved. And with each round of this over the years, I was consumed with one thing above all: when would I get the phone call that he died or was about to die? I ached to turn off my phone at night, to sleep fully undisturbed.

The night my dad died, I talked to Erica for more than three hours until about one or two in the morning. After we hung up, I finally indulged in what I had long yearned for, and I turned off my phone. I have always had a landline. So I just unplugged the jack from the wall and disconnected the phone itself and went to bed. I have done this every night since he died.

I just bought a new cell phone and had all the numbers transferred over. I noticed that under the letter *D*, I still have Dad listed as a contact; it's for his number at the nursing home. I still can't manage to delete the listing from my contacts. Apparently, this is a common response when people die. My colleague told me about how he spoke to his father every morning on the phone, and after he died, he still instinctively reached for the phone to call him.

I still want to call my dad, hear him answer and say, "Hello, Doodles," or "Hey, gorgeous." Just one more time. Maybe I would hear it differently or understand it in a whole new way, its cadence and rhythm, and savor it, knowing this was the very last time. No, actually, better yet, I want him to call me. To share with me something truly exciting going on, even at the end of his life. Hey, I'd even start plugging in my phone at night.

2

The Diaries

A dear family friend who is a bit older than I am often jokes that I was born in my midthirties. I have always been what you might call an old soul. At about age four, I dressed up for Halloween as a little old lady going to a meeting. At about that same age, as the story goes, my grandmother took me out for lunch, and I asked her in a voice that others around us could hear, "So have you read Lillian Hellman's *Pentimento*?" Not exactly children's reading in 1973. There are all the times when I was very little and my dad would order a vodka on the rocks or a scotch, and I'd ask for a sip and grab a hold of the glass with my first two fingers to get the strongest grip with my small hands. And then there's the photo that my dad took of me when I was about three years old, my hands clasped together, tiny fingers intertwined, adorned with huge rings, my chin resting on my hands, looking very solemn and pensive, staring into a coffee mug.

Sometimes, I think about these memories or look at these old pictures and wonder what that little girl thought of all she saw. I wonder how she knew what to remember and what to let go of in various moments. I wonder about her very earliest memory of the really bad stuff.

This little girl knew how to be super grown up. You learn that as an only child when you are thrown into adult conversations; you learn that when you are dying to grow up, dress up, and do big girl things. And you also learn that when you see too much. When you are exposed to violence growing up, you see too much. This little girl knew how to be angry and sad. She knew to be furious at her father when she was still very little. She also learned how to love him, and many other people, in big, epic ways. Somehow, she knew that she should put her experiences down on paper, have a place to remember how she felt about what happened to her. Even at age nine or ten, she knew that writing everything down would keep her honest about her memories, make her experiences indelible, render the circumstances even more real. It would make the stories shareable and less scary, and she would be less alone.

I look at this young girl's diaries now as an adult, the only two she ever kept, between 1979 and 1980. They were the size of index cards, with pink, flowery, slightly poufy covers and little metal locks on the side. Puffy stickers from her sticker collection were stuck on the covers, stickers with pictures of the sun and the clouds, butterflies and rainbows, smiley faces, and a few that say, "Keep out; top secret!" This little girl helps me remember.

January 2, 1979. We did a report in school, and my teacher hung it up on the board. I asked her if she really liked it, and she said she likes all my work. I was so happy. I'm really trying hard in school. Sometimes I'm a little nervous, but I'm really a good student. Also I really like rock 'n' roll! I really love Shaun Cassidy and Andy Gibb and Donny and Marie Osmond. My favorite movie is Grease, *and I have the record of it.*

When I read this now, I see a nervous little girl trying to please everyone.

January 31, 1979. Today I finished all my work. She said it was perfect! I was so glad! I love school sometimes!!!

Perfect was the only thing I have ever been able to strive for. I always wanted the teachers to notice me, to like me best. I understand better now how this tyranny of perfection lives on in women, especially those whose lives have been marked by trying to please people who couldn't be pleased, like my dad.

February 3, 1979. I went to Jill's party. I really don't like parties.

I still don't really love parties; I much prefer one-on-one interactions or very small gatherings.

February 16, 1979. We called my half-brother today to say, "Happy birthday."

I often wonder what it would have been like to actually *know* a sibling.

March 1, 1979. I was sick. I did not go to school. At least I missed gym. I also missed dictionary skills.

I really hated gym. I think I still harbor hatred for that gym teacher, a man who knew only how to nurture the talent of the kids already most athletically inclined. Maybe I was envious of those girls, like my friend Hilary, who seemed agile and gifted in every sport, because I could not compete and be perfect in this arena. And I might have been jealous of how those girls got to be so strong, so confident in their bodies. But the gym teacher didn't help those of us who didn't fit that mold to feel more confident. He left too many of us behind. I wonder how many of us ever found that body love on our own.

March 2, 1979. I was sick. I missed a spelling test. I'm real sad. I would have been the champ.

I was absolutely consumed with being the spelling and math champ in third grade.

March 7, 1979. Today I didn't go back to school in the afternoon. I went to the doctor. I don't know why I don't pray. I guess only Christians pray.

Even then, I questioned religion.

March 10, 1979. I wrote a beautiful story. It was my homework. I had no help. I got a memo pad to write poems on.

I always wanted to be able to write beautiful stories that others would want to read. And somehow, even at age nine, I intuited that I had something of value to write down and to own it as mine, without consulting with anyone and without adults checking over my work.

March 23, 1979. I have lots of homework. I hate when my dad falls asleep in front of the boob tube.

Since my mother never watched television and my father obsessively did, I experienced it as a tool of disconnection even as a kid. My reaction was an early sign of how much I would come to resent the television being used to monopolize a relationship in passive-aggressive ways.

April 16, 1979. I went out for another coffee ice cream soda. The glass was dirty with cherry gook all over it. Gross.

Big messes, small messes; they've always made me nervous.

May 6, 1979. I had a Z day [on a rating scale of A to F]. Everyone was so mad. Mom and Dad were mean to each other. My dad should be the one that should be blamed. Tomorrow there will be two math tests. I've been scared all day.

May 19, 1979. Sometimes I feel that my parents don't understand me. How come I sometimes have so many fears but I am a happy child? Maybe I'm sensitive. Sometimes there is nothing wrong with that. My dad left for a business trip in Palm Springs, California. I hope I'm the champ in spelling. But I hate studying for tests because it makes me nervous.

May 20, 1979. I went swimming. I did a somersault in the deep end. I miss Dad. I had an A+ day. I love swimming.

May 23, 1979. Only two more days till Dad comes home. I had a B day. But I got a card from my dad.

May 24, 1979. The boy I like talked to me. He is so cute. Dad is coming home tomorrow. I'm going to a birthday party tomorrow.

May 25, 1979. I went to the party. Dad came home. He got me lots of presents like swim fins and a visor and a bag and a circus book with a poster and a big history book.

May 27, 1979. My dad poked a knife near my face. But I said that I would forgive him. I had a B day.

I was trained early on to ride the cyclical waves of violence. I was swept up in the promise of seeing my dad return home, lured in by the excitement of his gifts and his love yet within two days of him being back feeling again trapped by his rage. The tyranny of perfectionism that I felt inside and outside my house was strangling, and I learned to ask, if only to myself, if I had done something, or forgotten to do something, that provoked him. He was always fast to apologize, and in turn, I learned to forgive quickly. I wonder how I could still rate the day a B when my dad did what he did.

June 23, 1979. I was so bored today. I have a bad cold. I don't think I'm breathing right. I sometimes don't think my mom and dad love each other because they have fights.

June 29, 1979. We didn't go swimming today. Tomorrow we're going to Lake Chautauqua.

In twenty-four years from exactly this day, I will get married to Mark. In thirty-one years from this month, I will tell Mark we need to pursue a divorce.

July 7, 1979. I called my father a bastard. I was really mad. He said I should forget about it, but it's the meanest thing I could ever say, and I am sorry. I love my daddy. He's the best.

I learned to apologize fast, sometimes even when I felt I didn't do anything wrong. I think that by encouraging me to forget about what I said, my father was banking support for when he wanted me to forget bad stuff he said and did. Swinging cruel words was like tap or jazz dance and forgiveness a sort of ballet.

July 19, 1979. Tomorrow Grandma Bertie [my dad's mom] is leaving to go back to Florida. In one way, I'm glad because she just sits around, and she doesn't even say anything about me, but she says something about Mikey and Raye. Those are her friends. Mikey is the grandson.

This grandma favored my cousins and her friend's grandson. I came in last, and I knew it. She was one person I knew I'd never please.

July 21, 1979. I went swimming while my mom and dad went to a wedding for my dad's secretary. Her name is Mandy. She is nice. She is pretty. A girl in my class is moving into the senator's house with a pool and tennis courts.

Noticing. Comparing. Growing up where I did, it seemed possible to imagine and believe that one day I would have all that too, however unrealistic.

July 22, 1979. I went swimming, and then it began to thunder. We left. I'm almost done with my book. I went to Nonnie and Poppy's [maternal grandparents] for dinner. We had cucumber soup, salad, lamb chops, baked potatoes, and ice cream. We played cards. Sometimes Poppy yells so loud, I hate it.

It was not until going back through my diaries that I remembered that my grandpa did this. I wonder if this is where my mom learned that this sort of behavior was typical in a marriage.

July 24, 1979. We had free swim in the pool. That was fun. Camp will be over in two days. I had a lot of fun, but I'm glad that I can be alone, having fun with my mom. I was safe when I ran to first base in kickball. I had an A– day.

I wrote the word "safe" six times in a circle around this particular entry.

July 30, 1979. I went swimming. I bumped into my mom when we were doing laps. She got mad and told me to get out. It was an accident, and I couldn't help it.

August 7, 1979. Tomorrow we will go to jolly old London. I am so excited. I wonder if I'll get sick on the plane. I probably won't.

August 9, 1979. My parents said the cab driver cheated us. We hate our hotel, and we're moving to another one. Hooray! I can't wait. I didn't start crying when Nonnie and Poppy left us at the airport, but I do miss them. I couldn't fall asleep. This is a secret, but I learned if you cry, it makes you fall asleep. I know it is strange. My dad was snoring, and my mom was asleep, so I was crying. I was a little upset because everyone was asleep and I couldn't get to sleep. I fell on a suitcase. It was so dark.

August 10, 1979. We moved into a new hotel. It's called the Portobello. It is beautiful. My mom and dad got into a fight, and I was worried. I started crying. I thought they were going to get divorced. I was afraid that I wouldn't be able to go to school because we would not have a lot of money. My dad said he hates my mom. They made up, but I'm still scared.

They even found a way to fight on vacation. Thousands of miles from home, this little girl felt dislocated, even with the only two people in the world who felt like home for her.

August 11, 1979. We went to the theater and saw Annie. *It was the best show. I loved it. We went to Hamleys, and I bought a peg doll. It is made out of a clothespin. It is cute! There is a man I saw who had green hair. It was gross. Sometimes I wonder if my dad compares me and his other two kids he had when he was married before my mom. I hope not. I don't like the idea that he had a girl.*

Here was one more place where I believed that worried perfection was the only path. With my paternal grandmother, I knew I was not the chosen one. But with my dad, the stakes felt even higher, and I wanted to be his favorite. As I grew older, my dad made it clear I was his only kid. Given that my parents stayed together decades more than he did with his first wife and that he and I were part of each other's lives until the day he died, he got a second shot of redemption with fatherhood.

August 12, 1979. We went to Hampstead Heath. I'm enjoying the trip, but the other ones were a little more fun. Sometimes I want something but I'm too embarrassed to ask. I hate having that feeling.

August 17, 1979. We went on a tour to Oxford. I don't like tours. We didn't get to do much on our own.

August 20, 1979. We went to Night and Day *at the theater. I hated it. My mom gets angry at me at night, and she says, "Go to bed. It is too late for a little girl." I can't stand when she does that.*

August 21, 1979. I'm always afraid to tell my parents something that they do that I don't like. For example, when they smoke and I tell them that it is bad for their health, they start screaming at me. I get irritated at them, and they get irritated at me.

August 23, 1979. The day after tomorrow, we are leaving London. I'm so excited to see Nonnie and Poppy. I'm sad to go back though. I know we'll come again. I hope. I've had fun. Today my dad blamed me because he fell on the bus all alone.

Unlike when I was nine, I no longer have the confidence that I will always get to return to a place I love. Now there's

the time bind, the money bind. This was our third consec-
utive summer going to Europe as a family. It became our
last. After that, we took some trips around the United States
together. The last real family trip we ever took for fun was
probably to New Orleans when I was in college. Once, in
graduate school, I met my parents in Philadelphia when I
was presenting a paper at a conference. I was twenty-five
years old—almost twenty-five years ago now. Four years
after that trip, they announced their divorce. My father and I
took a trip to Toronto in 2000 to celebrate his birthday, but
I never again got to travel with my mother except for one
long weekend to return to Cleveland. My mom and I talked
about taking more trips together, but it never happened. In
2004, my dad made elaborate travel plans to take Mark and
me to Delray Beach, Florida, over Christmas break. As he
was getting out of a limo to meet us at Cleveland Hopkins
International Airport, he fell on ice and broke his hip. We
never got to Florida. In fact, for close to eight years after that,
my dad remained stuck in beds and wheelchairs in Cleveland
until the day he died.

Unlike when I was nine and he fell while riding the bus
in London and blamed me, he didn't blame me this time.
But I blamed myself. I continue to, even to this day. I blame
myself for the fact that in the act of trying to take us on a
special trip, his whole body and life fell further apart. I never
apologized either because I never wanted to remind him of
what we had missed doing together. I live with this admit-
tedly warped but embedded belief that if he had never tried
to take us away on vacation, he would have never broken his
hip, and all would be well. Until it wasn't, since he was never,
truly, altogether well.

*August 24, 1979. When I woke up, my dad asked me if I wanted
anything because we are leaving tomorrow. I did want to go to*

the London Bridge, but we didn't have time. Maybe if we ever
come again, I could go. Sometimes I tell my mom things that Betsy
has gotten, and I sometimes think Betsy is spoiled. She gets Cal-
vin Klein jeans and an aquarium, a Gloria Vanderbilt sweater
and Gucci shoes and velvet pants. My mom told me that I am
spoiled too.

August 29, 1979. I went to the dentist's office. Dr. Cohen wasn't
there, but instead I had Dr. Goodman. I got the shivers when they
cleaned my teeth. He found a cavitie [sic], but the tooth will fall
out in a couple of months. He didn't fill it. Yeah! I got a toy there,
and I also got a toothbrush. Sometimes my mom asks me if I love
her. I hope she knows that I do. Sometimes I get angry at her, but
I still love her.

September 1, 1979. We went on Dick's sailboat, and we saw the
air show. I had so much fun, but then I went into my dad's arms,
and I hit my knee while he was holding vodka. I was scared. We
went to a baseball game. I ate so much. A lady got drunk on the
boat, and she asked my dad to neck with her.

Where was my mother? It's nerve-racking now to imagine myself scared on a boat with drunk adults, worried that
my dad would become angry with me if some of his drink
spilled.

September 12, 1979. I think my red lock is broken. Finally I got
it opened. I went into the gym autoortauiam [sic]. My eyes were
tearing. After gym, the teacher got so mad at me. He was yelling,
and I put the damn lock in wrong. I was listening, but I didn't
understand. I wouldn't dare tell him I did not understand.

This is that same fucking gym teacher from the previous
school year—the one who was great at humiliating you if

you weren't a top gym student. I learned to be good at hiding what I didn't understand. It always seemed easier than someone getting so angry at me. I've heard that teacher died; at least he can no longer mess with other young girls' sense of self.

September 30, 1979. My mom and me [sic] don't get along as well as we should because we argue too much. I sometimes get scared, and I think they'll lock me in the shower or give me away, but that would never happen. When we were on our trip in London, they always used to fight, so I thought they'd get divorced. They still fight with each other, but they don't fight as much.

I never really learned the difference between normal arguing and what is too much—what would finally rip a relationship apart, break open a family, leave a kid feeling that trapped or feeling that able to be discarded.

October 4, 1979. My dad always says that I should listen and not talk, and then when he is explaining something to me, I'm afraid to ask a question.

October 9, 1979. My mom and dad get angry at each other too many times. I read a book about a lady who got married, and then she got divorced and she married someone else. Her first husband bossed her around. I wonder how Mom feels about Daddy.

October 14, 1979. When I ask for help on my homework, I ask a question, and then my dad says don't talk, you'll never learn. Before he can understand what I need help on, I have to tell him and explain it to him.

October 15, 1979. One time I got scared he would get so impatient, I would have to tell Mom, and the next day Mom said, "You should ask me." I told her I was terrified.

October 24, 1979. I am embarrassed that I play school or house and I pretend Dan is my husband. I wonder if I will have a good husband. I wonder if I will have a boy or a girl. College is in nine years. I'm nervous.

This is what girls are socialized to do—to create and maintain relationships, to dream of weddings, marriages, and families. But why was I worried about college at age nine? Abuse, worry, and perfectionism all make it so hard to fully stay in the present.

October 25, 1979. I wonder if Mom thinks Dad is bossing her around. They fight a lot. I get scared. I couldn't ask Mom. Even though Mom and Dad say I can tell them anything, this might not be able to be asked or told.

This little girl sounds so eerily old. Somehow I intuited that in that space that alternated between rage and silence, transgressions were made that could not be spoken of.

January 28, 1980. Today my dad was sitting watching TV. The TV is behind my bedroom. I wanted to go to bed early because of the slumber party. I was in a pretty good mood. I went downstairs to ask Mom if I should ask him to go downstairs to watch TV. She said yes. I did. It worked out, and I told him the truth.

How sad that the unpredictability of my dad's responses meant that I had to ask my mom what I could ask my dad—that I sometimes needed her to run interference, even just to ease my mind. For too many years, it remained hard for me to ask or tell a man what I most needed and wanted.

February 28, 1980. My mom and dad got into a huge fight. Again. I don't really want to get married. They were calling each other sons of bitches. Ooh.

As most little girls at age ten dream of princesses and marriage, I was already bowing out, questioning what struck me as a most tenuous institution at best. And when I said, "Ooh," I think I sensed then how childish they seemed, how all the name-calling really accomplished nothing. And I think I didn't really believe them. I think I didn't really believe *in* them—in them together.

March 2, 1980. Nonnie and Poppy called! Mom grabbed the phone away. I really can't stand her anymore. I talked for one minute while Mom took up the whole phone conversation. I really miss them, and Mom makes it so much worse.

My mom often had trouble interacting with me against the backdrop of relationships with other people. Even when I was away at college and called home, if I was talking with her, she repeated yet distorted what I was saying so my dad would then hear something else, something he could question me about or get angry about. When she did that, she was able to temporarily get him to side with her. When I was home and I was talking to someone on the phone in my room, she would come in and insist on knowing what our conversation was about, assuming we were talking about her. She sided with my dad when he was being nicer to her and mean to me, and when he was being mean or threatening to her, she sided with me to have someone on her side, and maybe to protect me too. And my dad was never okay with being left out of whatever mother-daughter bonding we could muster, so even when I returned home from college and they picked me up at the airport, she would ask me questions or I would want to share stuff, and he wouldn't have it. He found all sorts of ways to drive a wedge between us. And he did. It was in his illness and in his death that she and I learned better how to talk with each other, how to be with each other.

March 3, 1980. Mom said she doesn't care if she dies. I think it is an awful thing to say. We went to Value City yesterday, and Mom was so impatient in the store.

My mom has always possessed a remarkable ability to shut out and shut down, and I think this comment, however reckless it was to utter to a ten-year-old on a mother-daughter outing, hinted at a longer struggle with anxiety, depression, and abandonment that I was not aware of until much more recently.

April 3, 1980. I ran away for five minutes. I even packed. Dad keeps saying, "If you do that, I will lock your bicycle."

April 17, 1980. Today I got home fifteen minutes late. Mom called me a little shit. I was so upset. Dad was angry 'cause I didn't put away my shoes, so Dad was having his temper tantrum and looked like he was gonna hit me. I was crying, and then Dad had a talk with me.

My father never hit me. But the perception that he could was always there. The threat was present, which actually felt scarier because it was always hanging over my head. Even at age ten, he looked to me like a child having a temper tantrum—a child who could hurt and bully me and make me feel bad.

I wonder what my dad and I talked about that day. I imagine he explained the situation back to me using abuser logic—if I had not been late and had put away my shoes, he never would have been angry, so ultimately it was my fault. But that maybe he overreacted and wanted my forgiveness. I wanted to be perfect in his eyes, wanted his approval, his love and his kisses, and his telling me everything would be okay, so I'm sure I forgave him—at least at that moment I probably did. But years of doing that too often culminated in years of me later realizing I didn't need to forgive him or to forget.

The last time I ever wrote in a diary was April 17, 1980. I think I've spent the past thirty-nine years trying to live and write truthfully out of that mess—living in some space between forgiveness and blame, between forgetting and memory.

Sometimes, still to this day, as I am driving alone, I imagine that seated beside me in the car is that precocious little girl who penned all these entries, with piles of ringlets on her head, huge, curious greenish-gray eyes, her feet not yet touching the floor, and I try to remember to ask her what she needs now.

If I am quiet enough, open enough, I might hear her whisper.

3

Messages

You were the most beautiful baby in the entire hospital nursery.

You ungrateful little bitch.

You could be president of the United States.

You think you know everything. What, did you go to Harvard Medical School or Columbia Medical School?

I'm gonna kill you.

August 20, 2000, left a voice mail for me after he returned from a volunteer session at a local domestic violence center:

I'm tired of your attitude. Ya know, you get angry at me because I volunteer for something that I thought would absolutely please you, but you went and got angry at me, Deb. I don't get it. I don't know how to deal with you. You said earlier today when we talked that you should've called the cops on several occasions when you lived at home. How *dare* you even *think* that? When were you *ever, ever* in danger? Yes, I've got a loud voice and a big mouth, but when were you ever in danger?

Sang to me, as a child and as an adult,

> I love you a bushel and a peck, a bushel and a peck, and a hug around the neck, a hug around the neck and a barrel and a heap . . .

Your mother is a slut.

Tell your mother she's still the most beautiful woman in the world.

December 20, 2008, said to me in the nursing home, "I was a mean, miserable bastard, and I don't know how Mom put up with me."

Overheard him telling my mother during an argument when I was a teenager, "You have a dimpled ass. No wonder I'm not as interested in having sex with you." (I thought to myself at the time, "I have a dimpled ass too. Who will think I am attractive?")

You're such a good friend to so many.

Why do you spend so much fucking time with your friends?

Oh just shut up, Deb.

Sang to me, as a child and as an adult,

> You are my sunshine, my only sunshine; you make me happy when skies are gray. You'll never know, dear, how much I love you. Please don't take my sunshine away.

Fuck you, you little bitch.

Answered the phone when I'd call, "Hello, gorgeous!"

I can't wait for us to go on this great trip together.

Nobody's going on this trip.

Why do you always have to go and spoil everything?

If only you had done _____.

If you just had not done _____.

Advice to me:
1. Reach for the stars and you'll never come up with a handful of dirt.
2. Remember, a bird in the hand is worth two in the bush.

You're a better speller than I am.

In an email to me in 2001:

> You are awesome! You have a full plate, but somehow you seem to get everything done—and done well. I can't believe that you're the woman who such a short time ago couldn't pronounce "store"—it was "tore" and smart was "sarmt," and you watched "Sesame Treet" every day as you called it because you had trouble with some *s* words, and now you're conducting professional meetings and counseling men and writing papers and you'll soon get your PhD. Wow! However (didn't you know there'd be a "but" or "however"?), I caught you in a misspelling. Check your last email to me. You spelled "accommodate" with only one *m*. Debbie, Debbie, Debbie. I have to believe that someone else wrote the email for you or your overwhelming schedule just got the

momentary best of you. Did you know that you can set up your computer to spell-check automatically before you send email?

When are you gonna grow up? When will you ever learn how to manage your time?

I am so impressed with you, so proud of you.

You little shit. You ungrateful cunt.

Just lighten up, Deb.

Sent me this note in 2002 upon hearing that Mark and I preferred to call our wedding a "commitment ceremony": "This 'commitment' business is so immature. When a man gives a woman a ring—especially a diamond ring—the entire world calls it an 'engagement.' And nothing you do will change the world's perception or definition."

In a birthday card from 1994, "You have the capacity to change much in a world that needs much changing."

Told my mom, an abstract painter and printmaker who has shown and sold her work internationally, "Why are you spending so much money on all this goddamn paint? Who do you think you are, Picasso?" Three weeks later, buys my mother a $950 Sonia Rykiel velour running suit as though she would ever exercise or even run errands in that.

You can do anything you set your mind to.

If you're not going to be a lawyer or a doctor, marry one.

Just soften up around the edges, Deb.

I'm not criticizing you because I find it to be fun. I am trying to be helpful.

Let's talk, Deb, just talk.

Why don't you just smile, Deb?

Why don't you act more like a lady, maybe talk a little softer, laugh a little less loudly?

We both just need to try a little harder.

You'd make my life easier if you'd commit suicide.

I love being your father.

You're the most beautiful girl in the world.

Have you gained a few pounds?

Wrote a letter to me and included the lyrics of an old song, "Button up your overcoat when the wind is free. Take good care of yourself. You belong to me."

Here's some money so you can buy something you like.

You're so careless, so reckless with money.

In a note sent to me at college,

Mom is really pissed that you'd spend sixty dollars on a bathing suit when she spends twenty or twenty-five dollars. So don't discuss this with her. I know I told you it was okay to buy a bathing suit, but sixty dollars is a bit much. So take this check and send Dillard's a check for the bill. You may keep the change because I love you.

In an email from 2001, "You are so thoroughly spoiled, so obnoxiously selfish, I could vomit."

I love you so much I could burst.

I wish you'd just get out of my life.

When are you coming home? I can't wait to see you.

Valentine's Day card, 2003, "On the day you were born, you stole my heart, and you've kept it ever since."

I miss you so much I could cry.

Letter sent on May 18, 1998,

> If you want to come home, please carefully consider the enclosed agreement that Mom and I drew up and let us know your decision. If you agree, please sign one copy of this contract and return it in the enclosed envelope.

Fuck you.

I love you more than any father ever loved any kid.

Okay, so what would *you* believe?

4

Accidents

Just the thought of the tuna sandwiches at Panera Bread makes me queasy. I remember them being sweet and tangy, the tuna mashed up just so. My father came to visit us in May 2004 at almost seventy-seven years old. He came alone, without a girlfriend. I was prepared—well, I was never fully prepared, since he took me by surprise in a different way every time we were together. He relied on me differently when he was alone than when he visited with someone else accompanying him on the trip. And every time he visited, I wondered if it would be the last time he could make it. Walking had become so difficult for him; it had always been hard . . . flat feet, bad hips, back, and knees. But it had become considerably slower—painfully slower. My father would rent a car and stay at the Westin, since it was the poshest hotel in our neighborhood. We agreed that after he checked in and unpacked, I would go to pick him up. The problem was that my dad was neurotic about using his cell phone to track me. My cell phone buzzed as I circled around the exit ramp to his hotel, but I did not answer for fear of contributing to his nonsensical monitoring—the relentless "Where are you? How soon do you think you will be here? Why is it taking you so long?" For too much of my life, I abided by his rigid time schedules, was swallowed up by his drawn-out rants, and then got sucked into his quick fixes and half-hearted apologies. His behavior often threw me into a time warp; this may be partially why today my own sense of time is distorted and why I usually feel there is never enough.

I stepped out of the car to greet and hug my father, acknowledging to myself that it was more what one does in these circumstances than what I actually wanted to do. After not seeing my father for months, I wanted to want to jump out of the car and into his arms, eager to have five days of unfolding fun and leisurely time expanse. But I couldn't; I was too nervous about saying or doing the wrong thing, worried I would somehow ruin the visit.

My dad said he was hungry, so we drove to the nearest Panera Bread. It was about 4:30 p.m. He claimed he had not eaten since he had breakfast in Cleveland, nearly ten hours earlier. He told me that at 7:00 a.m., he washed down pills with a glass of OJ and ate half of a dry bagel. My mind raced. I knew his stomach got upset if he went for long periods of time not eating and then suddenly started devouring food. And I knew why he felt motivated to starve himself.

My dad had a lifelong struggle with his weight. Marla, his girlfriend at the time, the one who was famous for consuming liquid lunches of martinis, said that she really wanted him to lose weight, and he promised her he would lose twenty-five pounds by July 10. The problem was that it was already May 20. That meant he would have to lose more than three pounds a week, and that seemed very unsafe. I knew my mother's longtime issues monitoring his weight and all the nights he plowed through half gallons of Pierre's Ice Cream. Afterward, he would always say that he didn't remember eating the ice cream.

Those years of my childhood foreshadowed my college life with my bulimic roommate, who like a savage, lonely wild animal, would routinely consume whole packages of cookies, quarts of ice cream, and bags of chips and then stuff the empty containers far down into the trash can, hiding all evidence of her most recent binge. This obsessive consumption cloaked in shame, secrecy, and silence in turn foreshadowed what it would be like living with my alcoholic college boyfriend later, who simultaneously hid how much all the alcohol cost and denied drinking as much as he did, until one night after classes, I came home and found him blacked out on the bed and our apartment smelling like shit; he had gone in his pants and smeared it on the walls.

Back at Panera, my dad and I ate our tuna sandwiches and drank lemonade and made small talk about the weather and the flight. This sort of light chitchat is what I think of as safe talk; it was only when we ventured into more important territory that talking got harder or even impossible. When we finished eating, we decided that we would take home the leftover half of my sandwich and then take a leisurely drive until Mark arrived home from work, at which point we would then all head out for a late dinner. My time with my dad was always marked by meals—the planning of them and the eating of them; making reservations at the fanciest, newest, and most expensive places that he had read about; canceling the reservations and rescheduling them; making numerous reservations for the same evening; and doubting the choice that ultimately got made.

We drove back through the windy and bumpy streets of Waltham as my dad laboriously pointed out the landmarks he remembered and the landmarks he anticipated seeing if we were to turn left or right. Most of the time, he was correct. His sense of direction was always exceptional, almost eerie, all my life. He would get to a new city and immediately have his bearings. His sense of direction gave me an uncomfortable sense of security. I was glad he had it, but it was also a way he wielded control. For example, when we were on vacation, far away from home, on the other coast or in Europe, and my parents would fight a vicious fight, my father would be able to storm off, insistent that he was right and my mom was wrong about whatever they were fighting about, certain that we wouldn't know how to get back. My mother, with no sense of direction at all except an inner compass of intuition and resourcefulness, would reassure me that somehow we would find our way back to the hotel, back to home base. Somehow, together, we would find our way back.

My father and I drove toward my apartment building, and in spite of his sense of direction, he said, "Are we close to Overland?" and I said, "Yeah, Dad, we are on it now; my building is right here, right before this parking lot." And he said, "Good, because I think I want to use the bathroom." And I said, "Sure." All of a sudden, he indicated that he really needed to use it. I remembered back to other frantic, urgent moments like this, so I sped the car up the driveway, into the small parking lot, and into my space. With my father, I could never move fast enough. I tried to think quickly, to be ahead of myself as to where my house keys would be, since they are sometimes in my coat pocket and sometimes in my purse. We got out of the car, me prepared to run toward the house to open it for him and to put lights on so he could easily get in fast, but disappointingly, he said, "Uh-oh, Deb, I think I just made in my pants."

Even as I write this now, I feel clammy and nervous and sweaty and gross, and my heart is beating fast. I really disliked having to clean up after my father as if he were a giant baby. My dad had another accident I also vividly remember. He was driving Mark and me back to the airport during one of our many visits to Cleveland. All of a sudden, the car smelled deadly, and he indicated that he had to go to a bathroom. We drove fast to a McDonald's, but it was not fast enough, and he had a bowel movement in his pants. When he got out of the car to use the restaurant bathroom, we saw the mess on the back of his pants.

When I was growing up, my dad was the only one allowed to have accidents and make messes. However, when Mark and I visited him at his apartment in Cleveland one February after the divorce, we noticed that his desk chair had stains on it, as did an area on his gorgeous silver-colored, five-hundred-thread-count bedsheet. The edges of the toilet also looked somewhat soiled. I was amazed walking around his house that he had put so much energy, time, and money into picking expensive furnishings that were now destroyed. My dad was critical of everyone else's imperfections for so many years yet in his declining state allowed himself to make many messes. His harsh critique of others was so sadly frequent that I saw my father take perfectly nice things or potentially beautiful moments and contaminate them. Something that was supposed to be celebratory he could spoil and make utterly humiliating, something relaxing he could easily complicate and make tense and nerve-racking. I used to feel this way when I ate with him at expensive restaurants and he slung criticisms as fast as he demanded a drink order. Those are the things I had the hardest time telling my childhood friends from home. They seemed to sense the tension, but they spared me the embarrassment of asking me about it.

Back at my apartment after Panera, my dad said that he did not want to come into our apartment because of the mess, so I ran in to get plastic garbage bags and to throw my tuna sandwich remnants in the fridge. In the midst of hurrying to get back outside to my father, I don't know why I was so determined to be sure that a sandwich that I was sure to never take another bite of was promptly and properly refrigerated. Getting the leftovers into the fridge was like agonizing over picking out just the right clothes to pack when you need to quickly leave town to attend to a funeral—worrying about nothingness. Worrying about all I could still control and keep neat and in proper form.

My dad was standing by the door in his soiled clothes, looking desperate and sad, like a six-year-old boy, toilet trained for half his life but still messing up occasionally. He came in, and I wished I had laid out plastic in a path on the floor leading to the bathroom. He went toward our bedroom thinking that was the direction of the bathroom, and I redirected him and thought, "Please don't enter my room, my space with my husband. Don't mess that up too."

Soon, the whole apartment filled up with a sour odor. "Where is my mother?" I remember thinking. But maybe the bigger question was where had my father gone? His white $200 sneakers were doused with diarrhea. His right pant leg was drenched, and I realized that too was diarrhea.

The next day, to quiet me, humor me, sustain me, Mark said—he always said the one thing that would make me laugh even when nothing could be funny—"You should be grateful he wasn't wearing shorts." But he also mixed that in with "Don't punish the guy" when I shamefully admitted that I had screamed at my father for listening to his good-for-nothing girlfriend about needing to lose weight.

It is just not cool to starve yourself, especially when it makes you sick. I was impatient with my father, fed up with being surrounded by people with bizarre eating patterns and sick relationships with food and their bodies. My friends have all experimented with the Atkins and South Beach diet frenzies and with keto, paleo, and shake diets, and I know my mother always recorded in little notebooks she kept in the bathroom how much she exercised and if she overly indulged in treats or was "good." I learned early on that morality and virtue were attached to food. I also remember her so dying to eat something decadent that she would chew it and spit it down the kitchen drain to avoid consuming the calories. And there are all my students through the years who have told me about eating no more than cucumber slices, frozen yogurt, and cereal and then vomiting in school bathrooms. It's as though everyone around me was trying to really control something else.

How ashamed my father must have been of this accident at my place. How angry and filthy he must have felt—angry that his body betrayed him, aging and shrinking in stature in front of his only daughter.

Our bathroom felt filthy, all the floors felt filthy, the car felt filthy, and I felt filthy. I stood there trying to assess the mess, planning how to sanitize. I made a mental note of all the things needing to be cleaned: the bathroom, the floors, the outside hallway in our building, my clothes, and the car, since I did not know when and where the accident had really started. I wondered how long I would feel so dirty and disgusting. Even after superficially cleaning it all up, would my house ever feel clean? Would I?

I told my dad that I would go to the Westin to pick up fresh clothes, and I offered to let him shower at our apartment, not that I wanted to. I didn't want him to get any more deeply into my space. But I wanted him clean, and I wanted to do whatever was necessary to keep him contained in the bathroom. I announced my plans through the bathroom door, half shouting and half trying to seem caring and compassionate. I rushed back to the hotel and hoped that in this post-9/11 age of massive tightening of security and surveillance, I would still be allowed into his room, since he had misplaced his key. I told the staff that my dad was sick and I needed extra clothes for him in the event we would need to go to the hospital. They believed me, and the well-coiffed front desk manager kindly escorted me to my dad's room. In this chaotic moment, I envied how she appeared so self-possessed, quiet, and clean. I whisked through my dad's room, gathered up clean white socks, perfectly pressed pants, and neatly folded underwear. I went into the bathroom to grab some more Imodium for him and stumbled upon Dulcolax amid his other toiletries. I started fuming inside. Dulcolax is a strong laxative. Of course he would shit his brains out on our ride home!

When I brought the clean stuff back to my dad, who was still in the bathroom of my apartment, he insisted on taking his soiled clothes back to the hotel in plastic bags in my car. By that time, I was already richly fantasizing about the "Superior" car wash at ScrubaDub, which would not just Armor All the dash but would also scrub the fabric.

I dropped my dad off at the hotel and returned home, wanting him to never again return to my house. It turns out he never did.

I didn't want any dirty particle to get on anything else I owned. So I stripped down and threw my clothes in the laundry. Naked, I neurotically cleaned every nook and cranny of that bathroom. I hauled out every product from under the shelf. Ajax. Lysol. Clorox. Windex. Anything that said antibacterial on it, whatever I could get my hands on to disinfect, to take away grime. I scrubbed the toilet edges and the sink where he had washed his shoes. I felt an intense need to shower. I would have bathed myself in Purell if I could have.

Mark offered to take out the garbage, but I felt he shouldn't; this was part of my family mess to deal with, not his. I was so ashamed that Mark saw the remnants of my dad's accident yet realized he got it; somehow, he understood. In 1995, he had watched as my father called my mother a cunt on her sixtieth birthday on what was his very first visit to Cleveland to meet my parents. He loved my mom. He looks more like her son than I do her daughter. And he *adored* my dad. Mark could forgive my father's transgressions because he didn't have the history that I did. But thankfully, Mark didn't forget the things my father did either. I wouldn't have wanted to be married to a man who would forget. He seemed to understand the context of my family, and he accepted all of us. Though we're divorced now, this acceptance probably remains Mark's greatest gift to me.

As that weekend unfolded, my dad and I argued each day about taking my car or the rental car; I was continually obsessed with an accident happening again in my car, even though I did prefer to be in control of the vehicle. Once, we took his rental to Portsmouth, New Hampshire, for a day trip. Mark was in the front seat for more legroom, and I was in the back seat. My dad and I got into an argument during the ride, and he turned around while driving seventy miles per hour on I-95, raising a fist at me, looking like he wanted to haul off and punch me. Mark admitted that this made him nervous, and immediately my dad became nasty and critical toward Mark, asking him impatiently, "Don't you *ever* have an opinion?" Even I had conflicting feelings about Mark's silence in the face of my father's tirades, about his possible complicity in my dad's bad behavior toward me. I wanted Mark to speak back to my father because I had grown up thinking that talking back meant you had a position, a stance, and at the same time, I didn't want him to talk back and possibly make the situation worse. Later that day, in what became a makeup dinner, my dad ordered fried crab cakes, martinis, and prosciutto and spinach pizzas, all of this on top of the huge caramel Frappuccino he drank a few hours earlier. He was like a child wanting more and more at a candy store or an amusement park, taunting his body with rich food that was bound to wreak havoc on his digestive system, and I remained nervous every time he ordered something else. When I asked my dad if he felt well enough to order what he did or to go for an outing that weekend, he got very angry with me and accused me of meddling in his affairs. He swore and screamed at me about this publicly. A situation like this inevitably happened every time I visited him or he came to see me. And in those moments, I wanted him to go away, to evaporate, to not be my dad. But I simultaneously wanted a relationship with him, a better one. What probably made me the craziest was that on the last day of our visits, on the way to the airport, either in Cleveland or in Boston, he minimized and mutualized everything. He'd say, "Well, we had such a good time except for a half hour. And if you would treat me better, Debbie, you know I will always do anything and everything for you."

I can neither fully forgive nor forget what my father did over the years. Later, in conducting batterers' intervention groups, my colleagues and I would tell the participants, "Understand that she may never forgive you. Only stay in the relationship if you can be nonabusive in the face of this dilemma." As I doled out this advice, something about it was reassuring to me also, validating. I didn't have to forgive. But I have always wondered what my relationship with my father would have been like if I could have forgiven him, fully, when he was alive.

Still today, I live on the precipice of forgiveness.

Mark never approached or talked to his father in quite the same way that I talked to mine. Generally, he seemed to laugh more with my dad. I wanted to laugh more with my dad too. I still try to reassure myself that it is okay that I didn't. Mark's ability to laugh more wholeheartedly with my dad mitigated the absence of my laughter. Maybe my dad didn't really notice it anyway. I painfully wish I could have loved my dad more purely, the way it seemed like I did when I read back over letters I wrote to him from when I was a little girl.

The reality is that once I was a young adult and more aware of what was going on, the purity of my love for my dad got contaminated. That's what abuse does; it spoils things. It makes a mess—a big, shitty mess that becomes hard to clean, hard to contain, and hard to cover for. I always wanted to want to run into his arms. Even today as I write this, I want that, though he is long gone. But for most of my adult life when he was alive, I think I just held him at arm's length. Perhaps many adult children caring for dying parents deal with this dilemma—how much to let the parent in, how much to keep the parent at bay. It is hard to get that close to almost-death, to anticipatory grief. When an abuse history is part of it, that push/pull with how to have healthy emotional closeness and distance becomes that much more intensified.

I am not sure I always loved my father unconditionally, although I wanted to more than anything. It's as though the love between us, too, became hardened and soiled. Nothing returns to its original form. Abuse guarantees that. I am reminded of this when my mother has pointed out in recent years, "If I hadn't married your father, I wonder what I would have been like as a person."

I used to work with a meditation teacher and therapist who once quoted Sharon Salzberg: "Cultivate a mind so full of love that it resembles space." I always found that saying beautiful and peaceful until I wondered how to apply it to my relationship with my dad. With a love for my father still so mixed, so confused, so chaotic, so torn, how would I ever achieve this spaciousness I so crave?

I feel like my sense of spaciousness will come when I begin to open to the fact that I must also be spacious to this—to giving myself permission to feel that tattered blend-edness and accept it in myself. I see fathers and daughters who look like they are having so much fun, and it makes me wistful. I think of the friend I have who sang and danced with her father at her wedding, and then he performed the ceremony for her and her partner. I think of other friends who danced with their fathers at their weddings. I know my dad would have loved to play that role in my wedding, but I didn't even want it, at least not at the time I got married to Mark. I think I was trying to keep my dad's presence to a minimum at the wedding. I was already hesitant about how I would feel seeing my parents at our first gathering after their divorce, with new partners on their arms. I wondered and worried about how everyone would behave. My parents had promised to be on good behavior in the past for other occasions and didn't necessarily comply. And many times my dad threatened to leave important events or to not even show up, and I certainly didn't want something that monumentally embarrassing at my wedding.

I was also a little concerned about what my dad would say in his wedding speech to us. He had made a big deal about writing it, and I knew how important it was to him. I knew it drove him crazy that we weren't calling it a wedding and were instead referring to it as a "commitment ceremony" and that we weren't calling each other husband and wife but instead used the term "partner." It turns out his speech was pretty great; everyone loved it, and most of all, Mark and I loved it. Of course, he found a way to tease us, to refer to Mark as my "committed friend." That got laughs. But I was so worried about how it would all go, if he would be appropriate, that I had trouble just relaxing and taking in his words. I think my reaction—my concerned anticipation of what might happen—will always make me sad. But all in all, his speech was beautiful. I know that because every year on our anniversary, Mark and I watched the video of that special day, and my dad's speech was always one of our favorite parts.

In some ways, I still feel bad that I didn't let my dad have that dance with me. It's that papa moment that many fathers want to share with their daughters, and I knowingly, purposely resisted and deprived him of it. At the end of his speech, he referenced a song from the movie *The Wild Thornberrys*. I had never even seen it, but my father always knew about pop culture way before I did. The lyrics he quoted were from "Father and Daughter" by Paul Simon:

As long as one and one is two
There could never be a father who loved his daughter more
     than I love you.

My dad shared that song with us while dressed in a crisp black suit and silk tie, meticulously put together and looking handsome. None of us had any idea how almost exactly eighteen months later, life would flip upside down so cruelly. How could we have known? My sense of what constituted a real mess, a terrible accident, shifted and changed each time my dad got sicker and each time he sustained a new loss—losing the ability to walk, drive, read, write, see, stand on his own, feed himself, have bladder and bowel control, live alone in his apartment, think straight, and remember. Soon, there were many more things he couldn't do than could do.

In 2008, five years after Mark and I got married, I bought the Paul Simon CD that included the song from our wedding. That summer, we drove out to Cleveland to see my dad, and I brought it to the nursing home. After dinner, we were in the family lounge. My dad was in his wheelchair, and I was sitting beside him on an uncomfortable couch. He recalled how when I was little, I always climbed on his lap and how he loved to pick me up and hold me and dance me around. So instinctively, I reached for the disc, put it in the CD player, and went to sit on my dad's lap—a little gingerly, because I knew he couldn't hold me the way he used to. And even on that floor, sticky from old urine and spilled drinks, we danced the dance he probably wanted all those years ago. The bigger truth is I danced the dance I had rejected years before yet worried I would someday want. Or need. And so I grabbed the opportunity while I still could. And Mark looked on lovingly. He got it. He understood.

I had the chance to dance with my dad at our wedding dinner in a world-class restaurant owned by a TV celebrity chef, when things were far less messy, less gross. It might have been easier. But instead, I chose to sit on my dad's lap in that hollow, bleak, increasingly frightening place, and we squeezed out all the fullness of that singularly bright moment. And this dance that was entirely unplanned—a fresh, new, beautiful accident of sorts—took shape and had meaning. It was here that I finally felt more space, more love, not just for my father but also for myself.

5

Sugar

As a young girl, I thought that candy just appeared in my father's coat pockets. One of the most exciting things in the world was going to the hall coat closet in our house to see if there were any surprises hidden in what we came to call the "magic pockets." I thought some sort of candy fairy made sure these treats were there for me. I felt special. Almost daily, I ran to the closet at night and first thing in the morning on weekends and dug my small hand into my father's coat pockets; I often found Bazooka gum or Reese's peanut butter cups or little Hershey's miniatures. I think I first believed the candy really just appeared there; then later, I just wanted to believe it did. After some time, I learned that there really was no equivalent of Santa Claus or the Easter Bunny for Jewish children like me, no one but my dad who kept up this sort of tradition.

I still yearn for the concept of magic pockets. I have even been known to hide extra cash or candy in my own jacket pockets so that the next time I wear that article of clothing, I will smile and be surprised. I think I am also hoping to reach in and find and touch my dad. Even when I was forty years old, I walked to my then husband's closet, where most of my dad's more beautiful shirts and jackets were stored. With my dad in the nursing home, Mark wore these clothes: the Zegna, the Brooks Brothers, and the Gucci. All these years later and Mark still does not know how often I used to stand at the closet, grabbing fistfuls of sleeves, smelling them, still hoping to smell my father, a scent that strangely took two years to wear off of these clothes—something that both frustrated me and endeared me. Mark also doesn't know that I used to go to the closet, crouch down to child's height or just sit down, reach my adult arm into the pockets of the Joseph Abboud jacket or the Burberry, expecting to find peppermint patties, Hershey's kisses, or at least the Bazooka bubble gum wrapped in those silly cartoons. I would come into contact with only empty pockets and feel that Mark had failed me. I didn't marry Mark to find my daddy—at least I don't think so and I really hope not—but I wanted one goody, one bit of sustenance my dad always gave me. I think I wanted someone who remembered how to surprise me and keep me running back for more. Don't we find lovers and marriage partners who help us complete the narrative of our lives? Don't the people who show up for us to love do so mainly because of our own yet-to-be-worked-out longings and desires? I think so.

I have come to understand that the pockets are a metaphor for my complicated relationship with my father. Pockets are places of storage. Places where we hide things. My dad was brilliant, funny, warm, and generous to a fault. My dad was unusually cruel, the epitome of a son of a bitch—quite literally, as you would know if you could have met my grandmother. The truth is he was all of this. The pockets, then, remind me of the deep, dark crevices of secrets, shame, and silence as well as the openings and possibilities of brightness, magic, and laughter—essentially, the always incomplete and conflicted narrative that accompanies an adult child caring for an elderly and ill parent who was abusive.

My dad lived in a nursing home about six hundred miles away from where I lived. In exchange for all the clothes with the fancy labels, my dad was on Medicaid and wore shirts stained with whatever slop happened to be the meals of the day. Some were his old shirts, the Ralph Lauren ones, marked, like they do at overnight camps the world over, with "J. Cohan" or "Cohan" or "James Cohan." Those found their way back to him; others were shirts he never owned that were accidentally transferred to him through the laundry service. Every four hours, they checked his glucose levels and gave him insulin coverage when he needed it. On the trays of food that came up from the kitchen, he often got cake-mix cake with too-pink frosting and colored sprinkles. This had to be the first time in his adult life that he regularly ate cake made from a mix; mixes were always against my mother's religion. He traded in his fancy George Jensen flatware and used what they had in the nursing home, that human warehouse, and he ate off the dusty rose plastic plates.

In the last nursing home, the one where he got kicked out for calling staff members n—s and then cock-sucking n—s, they snowed him so badly with drugs that he had tremors and could not feed himself. I went to visit him there for his eightieth birthday in September 2007 and was forced to feed him his birthday cake. It was Erica who recommended the bakery at which I purchased the oversized and fancifully decorated cupcakes that year. Ironically, though diabetic since age nine and more dedicated to caring for herself than anyone I know, Erica has a vast knowledge of the best baker-ies and dessert recipes. I schlepped to the bakery she claimed was the newest and most lavish, located in a ritzy, chichi mall that could only be called La Place in the well-manicured Cleveland suburb of Beachwood, a place so poorly named it is comical, with no beach or woods in sight. Though when I bought the cupcakes, I sensed some of what might be in store for me as far as feeding him his cake, I nevertheless got excited about purchasing and bringing over something colorful, whimsical, and magical, just like the pockets he left for me. I was even enamored of the festive cake boxes and ribbons and bags at the bakery. In all the buying, I neglected to see that feeding my dad could never be festive, and my god, it was anything but magical.

Holding forkfuls of cupcake to lay on his tongue, I kept rehearsing in my mind how the fuck we got there, to that nursing home, to that level of incapacitation. To my being so grown up that I flew back to my hometown, rented a car, stayed in a hotel by myself, and called Mark to check in and say goodnight. There I was in Cleveland, a place I could not feel more comfortable and uncomfortable all at the same time, a place flooded with a sense of home down to my bones, and a place that begs me to ask what home even means every time I set foot at Cleveland Hopkins International Airport.

How could it be that I was feeding my father birthday cake, the same man who years prior dreamed up the advertising slogan for that famous American sugary drink, "Hey, how 'bout a nice Hawaiian punch?" How could this be the same man who every year took me to Cedar Point, an amusement park in nearby Sandusky, where we rode wild roller coasters and indulged in pink-and-blue cotton candy, essentially inhaling the spun sugar—me dizzy with admiration for my adventurous and fun and very ambitious father, the one who accompanied me on the rides that my mother was too scared to go on or when she was too uninterested to even come with us to the park? How could this be the man who Federal Expressed to me shipments of my favorite heart-shaped chocolates wrapped in red foil every Valentine's Day? How could this be the same man who devoured Charleston Chews and Mallomars with my mother during the happy hours of their marriage?

When my parents divorced, my father was already seventy-two years old. Though never a cook of anything other than boiled hot dogs, egg salad, and matza brie during their thirty-two-year marriage, my dad took up a love affair with cooking and baking that all at once puzzled me and pissed me off. Why couldn't he have shared more of this labor and this love with my mother, who was quite an inspiring and creative cook? He enrolled in classes at a high-end cooking school and became most proud of his homemade chocolate chip cookies.

As I've mentioned before, my father indulged in nighttime binges of half gallons of his two favorite flavors of Pierre's Ice Cream: mint chocolate chip and burgundy cherry. I still cannot easily or comfortably pass freezer cases in Ohio grocery stores that carry Pierre's, since all I can think of are the dripping ice cream containers left out on the counter for my mother to find crusted over the next morning at 5:00 a.m., when she awoke to swim a mile or walk five miles. Those bright-red half-gallon cylindrical containers with the white stripes on the lid have come to symbolize only sugar-filled stupors of loneliness—for my father, for my mother, and for me.

It's not just these excruciatingly private memories of my dad that haunt me but also the embarrassingly public ones as well. Mark and I went back to visit my parents the summer before they split. One hot and humid evening, we joined them to meet my mom's childhood friend Nanci and her husband, Ivan, for dessert at East Coast Custard. This is one of those places where people have the flavors of the day programmed into their smartphones, everyone knows everyone, and people become fast friends in line, comparing notes on new and favorite flavors. That night, the line was long, and my dad grew increasingly impatient. I left for a minute to go out and ask Nanci a question and returned to discover that my dad had just thrown an ice cream cone behind the counter—not at a person, as that was my first question, but in disgust about a person. I was mortified. This was in public with our friends.

Back at the nursing home, I unwrapped the cupcake for my dad, watching him want to eat it, observing as his hands would not stay still enough to manage that, and I realized I would be feeding him; I took the fork so automatically. However, I never feed people; Mark and I chose to not have kids, and I can't recall the last time I helped feed a baby. Mark even fed our two cockatiels. Once, a dear friend was over at our house, and I forgot one of the bird's names. I was lucky to remember to feed myself between classes, and when we were married, we were lucky when I thought to cook for us before 9:00 p.m.; I was never interested in rigid schedules. Life is a journey to mother and remother our-selves, I insist. My old, dear college friend Julie, who is a geri-atric care specialist, is uncomfortable with the discussions of role reversals between adult children and their parents and analogies that older people become like children in these sit-uations. But sorry, Jules, they do. My dad was no more than a dependent, defiant three-year-old at a lonely birthday party, and I was his lost, sorry mother trying to make it up to him.

There is a terrible intimacy and tenderness in feeding a parent. My dad was a very involved father, maybe too involved, always attending events at school, always want-ing to take my friends places with me. He nourished me in many ways, maybe most obviously in my love for words, for arranging and rearranging them, and for gourmet food. It was only right to feed him back. He also fed me many words and lines over the years that did a great deal of damage, that were despicable, that I have tried to purge from my system. Others have hung in there residually, and I carry those with me in my work teaching college students about intimacy and violence. I decided that feeding cake to my dad was a chance for tender redemption—for him and for me.

After all, this was my dad, who was larger than life. Maybe many little girls think their daddies are larger than life. Sometimes we are even physically propped up to think so. During a recent trip to Portsmouth, New Hampshire, I stood in line to get ice cream, and I heard a little girl, about four, sitting atop her father's shoulders, patting him on his bald head, yelling, "Daddy, look! Daddy, remember that?" How I still often long to call out to my dad, to point to memories, to have us catapulted back to an easier time—when he could move on his own. But in reality, that time was not easier for me, for my mother and I often paid a price for his freedom. Rather than carry out violence, my dad threatened it, and the threat was all that was necessary. It kept us in line. It was enough to taunt and torment, to worry us into perfection, to make us think that if we could do it right—whatever it was at the time—we might avoid the promise of something horrible to come.

I still remember getting ready for the trips we took when I was a child. The night before every journey, my parents fought, and my father threatened not to go—even after months of planning and dreaming about all that we would do, whether it be a fjord in Norway, an adventure in Tivoli Gardens in Copenhagen, an excursion through the English countryside, whatever. No wonder I still to this day dread packing and going to airports so much. As a little girl, I would go to sleep, unsure if in the morning we would be going or not. Every time, we did go. But every time, I worried and imagined we wouldn't, that I would have to tell my friends why we stayed home. As an adult woman, I rarely sleep the night before a trip, even if the plane is due to leave late in the day; I must be unsure if I will really be going and if I really want to. In the days before a trip now, I typically wake up disoriented and unsure of what day it is and unsure of whether I already went or will be going. Once on vacation, my parents routinely argued, and my dad would threaten to return home alone. We went to Paris in mid-July 1978, and my parents had a bad fight that started in a restaurant and then spilled out onto the street, and my dad threatened to take the next plane back to Cleveland and leave me stranded in a foreign city with my mother, the most directionally challenged person in the universe. Trauma challenges our sense of interior and exterior geography and disrupts our sense of place.

During those years of caregiving for my dad, he shrunk—first, in his physical stature, then in his cognitive capacity, and finally, and maybe most importantly, in my mind. Eventually, he lacked the ability to make compelling threats and actually hurt me. I would sometimes look at him in the wheelchair and think to myself, only half-satisfied, "Dad, bet ya can't get me now." But I lived with the possibility that he could and would get me, not because I wanted him to but because that is what I knew for so long. I always lived inside a contradictory reality of absolutely adoring my father while simultaneously being scared of him. How might I possibly let go of my understanding of my father as an abusive man? Do I even want to? Isn't part of the narrative of my life and my own healing firmly and squarely planted in this rendering of him?

For many years, my dad did things to keep me feeling small and to keep himself seeming large and in control. I recall celebrating his seventy-third birthday in Toronto, a trip he wanted me to accompany him on, as it was his first birthday after his divorce from my mother. Interestingly, Toronto is also the place he took me when I was about nine years old for a father-daughter weekend while my mother prepared for her first big art show. This was the second time I had my dad all to myself for days on end. I loved that as a girl, but this time, as a young woman, it worried me. I was thirty years old with him on the adult version of our trip, but it was like that nine-year-old girl was there as a third wheel; she was still with us everywhere. My dad constantly reminded me of how, during our first road trip there, I looked up at him with sheer joy when he pointed at our luxurious hotel; apparently, I couldn't believe we were staying at such a place, and I nearly jumped in his lap in the car. This trip, he decided to wow me with front-row seats to *The Lion King*. Truly, the seats and the show were spectacular, but this time my view of my dad treating me was tainted—on the one hand, I was ecstatic and felt special, and on the other hand, it seemed like a desperate attempt to show off and then to decide I was not grateful enough because my response was somehow less exuberant than when I was nine. I sat in the theater wishing I could still be this little girl for him, the one he relied on to look up at him, to need him. As a child, I used to say, "My daddy would do anything for me." As an adult, he often repeated it back to me as a way, I think, to remind me of his efforts and to assert his place in my life.

At dinner before the show, my dad said, "I just wish you'd tone down your voice, Deb." Minutes later, I was giggling about something, and he said, "I just wish you'd tone down your laugh, Deb." Now, this translates to me as "You need to shrink, Deb." His message was to be small, be quiet, be seen but not heard, be feminine, and take up as little space as possible. The lesson from my dad for how best to be around men came to me loud and clear both during the trip and in the weeks leading up to it. A few weeks before we went to Toronto, my father sent me a clipping from the *Plain Dealer* about how women should let men pay for dates. He enclosed a letter with the article in which he wrote to me, "The guy should pay, while the woman gets to look beautiful and makes the man happy that he's with her. So go for it, baby. Keep that purse closed and your lipstick creamy and fresh, and life will be good for you. Don't hesitate to show this to that loser of a Red Sox fan [Mark]. He's a really nice guy, but he doesn't know diddlysquat about who to root for or treating a lady. I'll give him lessons because you know how well I manage women."

I think maybe we need our parents to be larger than life for a good portion of our lives. And then, I think, they have to shrink in stature in order that we may grow. I believe this to be especially true for those of us who witnessed violence. My colleague and friend, a man named David who does domestic violence trainings all over the world, routinely shares a personal story about his own father. His father worked in the granite quarries in Vermont, and one day when David was four years old, his grandmother took him there to see his dad, pointed down, and said, "Look, David, there's your daddy." And David's grandmother recalled that David responded, "No way, that's not my daddy. It can't be. He's bigger than that." David did not recognize his father because down in the quarry, his father looked so tiny, like a dot on a gigantic landscape. To David, like any of us who witnessed and experienced violence, his father was huge for so long, mainly because the force and domination he wielded produced so much fear. When survivors of violence can begin to see an abuser's true size relative to the larger world, the abusers become less scary and more human. But with that new-found humanness comes newfound fear, the fear of which memories we are entitled to hold onto and which we must let go. And I have worked in the domestic violence field too long to truly believe in forgiveness. Redemption yes, maybe, but forgiveness no; it is so wildly overrated.

When my father was incapacitated and in the nursing home, I was aware of the fact that I could have made threats to him. I could have left him stranded; I could have finally taken sweet revenge and hurt him. But the reality was that I no longer wanted to do any of that. So the newfound terror I began to live with was the uncomfortable freedom and safety in knowing that at any point, I could walk away from him at the nursing home; I could get away from his antics, and I didn't have to go back.

Yet I always did. For another of my dad's birthdays, I baked lemon cake that I brought from Boston and took through security as carefully as a newborn. I used the recipe he loved, the one from my mother. Finally on less medication and able to feed himself, he tore into the cake with fingernails that had not been cleaned in weeks. But at least I was glad to not be feeding him. As a little girl, my dad's hands always looked big and strong, and I felt happy when we got along and my tiny fingers were enveloped in his hands. In the nursing home, even his hands looked lonely—no thick gold wedding band, just ground-in foodstuff from the week's meals.

I anticipated, and then worried about, my own soon-to-be bare left hand, the sparkling platinum diamond ring that I would need to remove once my divorce with Mark became finalized—a divorce I had wanted and asked for. I dreamed about selling the ring and taking the money to pay off some of my graduate school loan debt—debt my father hoped to help me with before he wound up falling and breaking his hip on Christmas Day 2004. He then needed around-the-clock care at home for years, which led to the draining of all of his finances and going on Medicaid.

As we negotiated the divorce, I tried to convince my mother and an attorney that while symbolic, the ring did not matter, that it was just stuff, but seeing my father's hand made me realize wedding rings are loaded with more than that. They signify you were one of the chosen ones. Vetted. And if you are young and wearing one, you reveal that you likely got picked on the first go-around. At age forty, soon to be without a ring, I imagined I would look picked over.

When I'd get my nails done, I'd see women all around me, most of whom were wearing elaborate, gleaming rings, and my mind took me on a journey into their perfect, clean marriages and lives. Lives I assumed to be refined and luxurious, evoking ease and the good life. I knew intellectually that any of these women could assume the same of me. It is like we wear these bands and are part of the Seemingly Perfect Club, the Perfect on the Surface Club. A great line from one of Tracy Chapman's songs haunts me: "There is fiction in the space between." It seems we have all bought into a sort of marriage shutdown syndrome. When we are newly involved with a lover, we reveal a lot about the person to others, and we constantly want to talk about them. But then we marry, we inevitably fall into places of tension and conflict, and we become more reticent to share that stuff. We wind up sometimes colluding in our own homespun pain. This, at least in part, is why it took my mother until age sixty-four to finally leave my father. I am sure she left him many times before that in her head.

I watched my dad consume the lemon cake for the three days in a row that I visited for that long birthday weekend. I wished I could bake and cook more for him, but I always stayed at a Courtyard by Marriott with not even a dorm fridge. And in reality, I probably should not have even brought birthday cakes. I rationalized it by telling myself it was his birthday. But after all, my dad was diabetic. I got my middle name from my father's father, who had his foot amputated a year before my birth from complications from the same cruel disease. Several times a year, I compulsively ask doctors to administer glucose tests to me, just in case. I get it; I know the risks. But I just wanted to indulge him—and myself—with familiar food.

My dad didn't seem to care. He was routinely given packages of Nilla wafers and Lorna Doone cookies, bags of cinnamon Teddy Grahams, and 3.6-ounce cartons of orange sherbet and vanilla ice cream, the kind that mothers buy for their three-year-olds for nursery school birthday parties. This for a man who thought not even Godiva was decadent enough. At the nursing home, morbidly obese nurses threw him these treats as though he was a zoo animal. These women, who looked like they didn't know the first thing about caring for themselves, were caring for my father. I was at once grateful to them and simultaneously sickened by the twisted ways care was constructed at that nursing home. And I worried about these women loaded down with weight, a heaviness oftentimes brought on by trauma. They wore a certain body armor, a signal to not come too close because someone already did who shouldn't have. I became that much more grateful to the black women caring for my father for they endured a special blend of sexism and racism, as he called them black bitches and fucking n— cunts, and they *still* cleaned his white ass. I worried, then, about what they cleaned up at home. A mark of womanhood seems to be cleaning and clearing—often other people's messes, and yes, especially men's.

The visit for my dad's birthday wound down. By Sunday afternoon, I needed to get back to the airport to catch my plane back to Boston. My dad asked, "Honey, can I drive you back to Boston and finally see your house, and I can fly back?" This, to anyone looking from a distance, would have been funny, if only in its painful absurdity, as my father was losing his hearing and eyesight, could not get out of the wheelchair by himself, and was completely incontinent. This reminded me of a conversation I had with my old flame and college friend, Tom, who claimed that we'll know we have dementia one day when we start rambling on about adventures at the circus in Egypt, the sort of stuff our grandmas uttered when they rapidly declined.

But the odd part is that my dad's idea was completely in character, something he would have certainly offered years earlier, when he drove a big black Toyota Avalon sedan with tan leather seats and a sunroof, a car that screamed geriatric pimp, but he loved it. And my father had always said that his dream before he died was to see the house Mark and I created; we bought a very old colonial and completely gutted and renovated it. We embarked on that effort almost five years after I dismantled my childhood home and very near the time I moved my dad into a nursing home and emptied his apartment, the one he had moved into and lavishly appointed right after the divorce. Feeding cake to my father was akin to taking apart those homes and his life as he—and we—had known it. It was seeing stuff I wasn't supposed to see, being privy to stuff I should have never known. I didn't have the heart to tell my dad that Mark and I would be divorcing, that even my time remaining in that house was going to be stunningly abbreviated. My dad adored Mark, saw him as the son he got to finally have a relationship with, and he would have probably intuited that some of my own need to leave was familiar to why my mother left him. I told my dad it was okay, that he should stay and rest. He looked at me quizzically and said, "So, Deb, did they take my car?" And I said, "Dad, remember, we had to sell your car a few years back when you moved here." And then amid the dementia but with some obvious lucidity lurking about in there somewhere, he said, "It feels like they have taken everything from me, and the worst part is they have even started to take my mind."

Months later, back in Boston, I was cleaning and clearing—closets this time. In preparation for the divorce and my eventual move, I was trying to get rid of old clothes, the ones I had not worn in years or that were no longer beautiful and functional. I've always been neurotic about my closet; all like items are hung together and then arranged in color order. I came across the cardigan section. Peeking out beside the others was a white cotton cardigan hoodie sweater, the last article of clothing my father ever purchased for me, back in 2003 before his fall. After that, he occasionally sent me money so I could purchase a new coat or new shoes, because he always said he wanted me to be warm. But the white sweater was something he bought for me, in front of me. His attitude in a store was "Honey, if you like it, buy it." I've had the zipper fixed on that sweater at least three times. The tailor repeatedly tells me that it is not worth it, that replacing it with a new sweater would be cheaper, that again, it will never hold up, and besides, there are a few coffee stains on the elbow because sometimes I can be a real slob. But I always insist on repairing it. I spare the tailor the details. I don't have the heart—or really, the courage—to throw it out. If I toss it, I will have discarded part of my father, and maybe as I see it now, the part that has the most to still teach me, about what we hold onto and what we let go.

Oh, and besides, that sweater has pockets.

6

The Dinner Table

In the spring of 2013, I taught my Intimacy and Violence class to twenty-eight students at the university. We discussed the connections between a variety of readings and video material, and one of my quieter students, Neil, observed, "It seems to always come back to the food." He had a point, I think. I had shown the class a public service announcement in which a man is abusing his wife and berating her for serving pizza while a child sits nestled in the spindles of the banister listening and frightened. I had also shown them a gritty feature-length film in which a battered woman gets so angry at her abusive husband and his friend when asked to cook eggs that she throws the eggs on the floor in a moment of resistance but minutes later is brutally attacked and then raped. And then there was the story I shared about a student I advised several years back who wrote in her senior thesis about an abused woman she had interviewed who tried to make it on an allowance her husband gave her, so she got into the habit of replacing the Heinz ketchup bottle with generic, cheap ketchup. One day the husband learned of this and began to beat her up and threw her and the kitchen table across the room.

One of the most gruesome memories I have related to food and violence was when a student named Carla met with me during office hours and told me that our class was hitting very close to home. This part is typical; I hear this a lot. Then she recounted how, as a young girl, she overheard her stepdad making demands of her mother—"Open your legs, damn it. Open your legs"—and how her stepdad came to Carla's room when he was finished with her mom. For the next invasion. She told me how angry she was at her stepdad but maybe equally angry, if not more, with her mother, claiming, "Deb, my mom pimped me out." And then she told me that her stepdad made the kids kneel on uncooked rice because it was sharp and would hurt and then made them eat food they hated and feared. She said she despised tomatoes, and she was made to eat them until she threw up, and then she was forced to eat the vomit.

Maybe Neil was right; maybe there's something about the food. Or maybe not the food per se but the meanings we attach to it. The daily acts of shopping for food, preparing meals, cooking, sitting down to eat, cleaning up, or dining out can be intimate or distancing, forging both connection and disconnection. Loaded on our plates are not just the foods we consume but also our feelings, sometimes the trauma of memory and sometimes the trauma of grief. Or sometimes humiliation and punishment are scooped onto our plates, and we have to consume that too. We wind up eating our hurt, our pain, our conversations, both the ones we had and the ones we wish we could have. We eat our silence, others' silence, our losses, our loneliness, and our dread. We eat our longings and our worries, our hopes and our fears.

I often find myself saying to students that trauma lives in the body on a cellular level. Losing my father has taught me that grief also lives in the body on a cellular level. I have come to believe that grief has a taste and that sometimes it even has the taste of not being able to taste. Perhaps trauma has a taste too, and sometimes the taste of not quite being able to taste.

I know connection has a taste. On menus, I see omelets with American cheese and think only of Hope, my friend, who met me for years at the S&S Deli in Somerville, Massachusetts, for breakfast food served all day, what I regard as the perfect menu, and then we would walk for hours, figuring out our lives. I see butter pecan ice cream and think of my mom's mom. I don't like butter pecan ice cream, but my grandma loved it, and so I think of her whenever I see it. She made tongue sandwiches for my grandfather to take to work, and though those sound far more disgusting than butter pecan ice cream, I see them on deli menus, think of her devotion, and smile. Just like my mom's response when she sees pears for sale in the grocery store. She doesn't even eat pears, but her father loved them, and she loved her father, so the pears become sweet, they become beautiful. Erica and I still talk about the biscuits and the whipped, salty-sweet butter they served at the Cooker Bar & Grille and those divine thick wedges of fried zucchini dipped in ranch dressing. To this day, when I eat biscuits or zucchini, I think of her and those leisurely lunches we had on our breaks home from college nearly thirty years ago.

I tried oysters for the first time with C. J., one of my favorite human beings in all the world and the man I am sure I would have married if only he liked girls. He came to visit me in Boston just a few weeks before I moved to South Carolina. We meandered through the South End and first got decadent chocolate brownie–like cookies at a tiny bakery; I guess we sort of ate backward that day. Then we stumbled upon B&G Oysters, where we sat at the bar, and he taught me how to order and eat the mother ocean. I had never before even wanted to try oysters. They seemed slimy and slippery and generally unappealing. It was with some trepidation that I put them in my mouth. I sucked off the salt and loved them. I think I was just ready to taste something new. I was just about to leave the home I had shared with Mark after two years of living together after our divorce, an odd arrangement at best, and one that made me feel stuck at worst. Food takes us back, yanks us back, but it also moves us forward.

I know a couple whose daughter was murdered by their son-in-law, stabbed sixteen times coming out of a shower, and every year on her birthday in early November, they eat her favorite meal of veal marsala and pecan pie. Writer Ann Hood, in her book *Comfort: A Journey through Grief*, talks about how she eats sliced cucumbers and shell pasta with parmesan cheese to honor her daughter, Grace, who died at age five of a virulent case of strep throat. I hear these stories and find it endearing and moving that people remember their loved ones through food. It's the way we toast the people we wish we were dining with, bringing them back to the table through their favorite foods.

But somehow, I have a harder time doing that. When I think of my dad and food, it's complicated. On my trips back home to Cleveland, before my dad moved to the nursing home, he always anticipated my visits weeks in advance and asked me what sorts of special foods I'd want. Returning from the airport to the house, I always found an overabundance of food in the fridge and the freezer—he had carefully and thoughtfully shopped for so many of my favorites. There were whole watermelons, a variety of sorbets and frozen yogurts, fresh bagels and lox and cream cheese, and colossal Bing cherries. Everything was oversized, like the roses he'd send me on my birthdays and Valentine's Day that looked like they were on steroids.

This supersized perfection made me all at once giddy and sad; my dad's heart was full of sweet anticipation for me, and I knew that and even still know that. But the history of our visits told me that there would inevitably be tensions and issues and that when I would displease him, as I somehow always managed to do, he would use these purchases against me, calling me insatiable and ungrateful, recounting all he had done for me. Sometimes the oversized look of it all mirrored how oversized his love for me seemed—not in a good way, but in a smothering way. When I came back to Cleveland, I also wanted to see my old, dear childhood friends, but he was critical that I saw them too much, that I hadn't reserved enough time for him. I often felt contained and even detained by my father many times as a girl with an emerging sense of self. My dad's love had a way of being claustrophobic. Not just because he was so controlling, but because his way of expressing love was blurry and confused.

Claustrophobia is the antithesis of freedom. This claustrophobia meant that I had less space than I needed, and the saddest part is that as a result, he created less space for me to love him back. Oh, I loved him, I really loved him, more than I can describe, and I still do, but I think I could have loved him better than I did. Notice I didn't say more, just better.

The other snack my dad always had on hand were bags of Snyder's pretzel rods, which he stashed in the pantry. He adored those things, so much so that when he was sick in the nursing home, I brought him a few bags during each visit. We'd suck the salt off of them, especially savoring the burnt ends. I can't eat those now. I still buy pretzels. I still eat them—the minis, the sticks, the thins, the braided sourdough ones, the nibblers, the spoon-shaped ones, any of them, just not the rods. Pretzels are a great road trip food, and Mike buys them to snack on with Diet Coke, liking how the salt of the pretzels melts with each swig and swish of the soda. One day, at a convenience store very early on in our relationship, Mike reached to grab a bag of pretzel rods, and I immediately said, "Oh, wait, sorry, I can't eat those." He didn't understand at first, since he had seen me eat pretzels. As irrational as it seemed, I explained, "See, it's that shape I can't eat. It was my dad's favorite." It seems so ridiculous, like a kid who gets hysterical if different foods are touching on their plate, but he knew better than to laugh at me. He just simply stated, "Sure, I understand," and instinctively reached for something else. Since then, we have bought snacks in gas stations and grocery stores, and whenever we decide to get some pretzels, I have signaled to Mike, "You love the pretzel rods, just get those." But he's too kind.

My mother tells me she has the same problem with apples. One day we were talking on the phone as she was eating an apple. She eats one every day after lunch. She prefers the ones that are tart and crispy, like Pink Ladies, claiming Red Delicious and Golden Delicious are like potatoes and McIntosh are far too boring and pedestrian. She started telling me about her new favorite apple she just discovered—Sweet Tango. I asked her, "Mom, have you tried Winesaps?" And she got choked up and began to cry. "Honey, I can't eat those. They make me too sad. Every day for eighty days when Poppy was in the hospital, I brought a Winesap apple and a knife. I'd ask him, 'Daddy, do you want some apple?' And he'd say he'd have a little, and I would cut him a piece, and we'd sit and share an apple and talk. Thank God they don't sell them around here so I don't even have to walk by them in the store." I told her I understood, that while some people find comfort in foods like this, to me, they become too hard—too sad—to eat. She went on to say that she doesn't feel like that about all foods when she thinks of her parents. I agree. I am the same way. My mom described how when she was a little girl, her mom made blintzes, and she still loves them and regards them as the ultimate comfort food. I have come to think it's about when and how and in what context we shared the food with the people we love. When I brought bags of pretzels to see my dad in the nursing home and when my mom stashed apples in her bag to see her dad in the hospital, these weren't days of happy food memories. These were intense days of caregiving punctuated by moments we tried to make better, more normal, more palatable, for our parents and for ourselves. Who would ever want to taste that again, devour it whole?

The first time I went back to Cleveland to visit my dad after we had moved him out of his apartment, when it was clear he would be living in the nursing home until the day he died, I realized he would no longer be asking what I wanted him to buy for my arrival, he would not have made reservations at the new, swanky restaurants or my old favorites. We wouldn't get to talk about the funky restaurant logos; the beautiful, creative fonts on the menu; the cool design of the restaurant space; the inventive mixtures of ingredients; the way the food was presented. There were no more free tickets to shows and concerts and baseball games that he used to get from television and radio stations, events where we'd eat rich, decadent junk food. It was like all the best food died.

I moved from this image of a man who used to adoringly guzzle down Bombay Sapphire martinis straight up with jumbo olives stuffed with pimentos, who always ordered extra olives to give me since I love them, to then being fed thickened liquids, with a nectar consistency to prevent choking. He never once said he missed those martinis or asked for them in the nursing home, but I missed the man who could order them.

When my dad first moved into his apartment after the divorce and bought every new mini–kitchen appliance one never even uses, he kept saying that he wanted to host a big dinner party. He never did. But his interest in—really his obsession with—good food was evident in so many ways. People always remarked that given his writing talent and his foodie sensibility, he would have made a terrific food critic. It's true. He would have. When his friends and colleagues told him they were planning a trip, he loved being the one to send them lists of restaurant recommendations and the best menu options at each place. He enrolled in a fancy cooking school, bought Mark Bittman's *How to Cook Everything* and other specialty cookbooks, got subscriptions to *Cook's Illustrated* and *Bon Appétit*, and searched online for recipes in the middle of the night. If Yelp or Trip Advisor had been popular before he got sick, he would have loved them. He would have Yelped himself silly.

I have all this stuff now. In my house are stored the cookbooks, magazines, and printed recipes; I have never cooked anything from them. I have the manila folder of the recipes he most loved and recommended, marked with his revisions. I imagine a time where we might have been able to cook together. It sounds momentarily fun, and then my mind goes to how he would likely get impatient, mean, and critical. I look at the recipe for stuffed salmon with crabmeat and spinach and the one for his famous crab cakes, and I'm curious; I think I should probably try my hand at these. And yet I still cannot take myself there, not to that food. At least not yet. I keep asking myself, "For whom, for what, shall I make space at my table?"

The idea of who and what would show up at the dinner table has long consumed me. When we were married and were looking for a house, Mark and I decided we wanted a dining room. Not an eat-in kitchen, but an actual designated dining room. Not necessarily a very formal one, but a real one. To me, it signified something about a warm, festive house. We fantasized about purchasing a very contemporary

Italian dining table in a rich wenge wood with extendible leaves and tempered glass with a frosted finish. We already had everything we wanted to put on the table. There were the curvy, colorful candlesticks we had longed for and gotten for our wedding, we had the shiny silver platters and salt and pepper shakers and napkin rings and some gorgeous hand-painted ceramic pieces. We were outfitted for exquisite dinners alone and with friends. Yet we were never able to afford that table. And when Mark's parents moved from their home to senior housing, we got their table and chairs, a traditional cherry set that they had used for Shabbat dinners and other religious holidays, set with kosher plates.

Their rules and rigidity around food were foreign to me. I admit that I probably have more resentment for the practice of keeping kosher than is warranted because of my relationship with Mark's parents, but really, I can't understand all the finagling of the rules, like bringing in Chinese food and eating it on paper plates in the living room so it never enters the kitchen, or waiting six hours after eating meat before eating anything dairy, or being willing to eat at a pizza place but only ordering cheese pizza when you actually eat meat otherwise. All the hypocrisy and manipulation around food made no sense to me.

Since I didn't have great memories of fun meals at their house, I didn't particularly want their table. I remember one particularly bad party—a combined Chanukah and birthday celebration for Mark and his twin brother; they were born on December 16, so we celebrated both occasions together at their parents' house. After we ate the bagels and lox and frozen potato latkes, we then had ice cream cake for dessert, for their birthdays. And no one bothered to check in with Mark and his brother about their favorite flavors of ice cream, so they got boring chocolate and vanilla.

Their mom put the cake on the table, and then their dad started to light the candles and sing for their birthday. The only problem was that Mark's twin was in the bathroom. That moment told me everything about how birthdays were handled in their house, and it signaled to me a certain sort of alienation around that table that gave me pause for later having it in our home. But it was the only reasonable and practical way to make the space a dining room where we could actually sit down and eat.

I am not sure how that table won out and why we didn't use my grandma's table, the one I had eaten at all my life and the one that my mother had eaten at when she was a little girl. I think it was because at the time we moved to the house, I had a fantasy of doing my work at a huge farmhouse sort of table, one that would be like an enormous writer's desk with just my laptop, a few tablets of paper, and a colorful pail of sharpened pencils. That felt creative to me. So we had my grandma's table put upstairs in my home office.

Other than a dozen or so dinner parties for friends and one Thanksgiving, we never used his parents' table and chairs or even that dining room. Mark and I wound up eating almost all our meals, when we ate them together, in front of the TV, trying to balance plates on our laps, actually juggling a relationship that was, for too long, hanging in the balance. Now when Mike and I make dinner, I ask where we should sit to eat it, at which table—the one in the dining room or the one in the sunroom or possibly even on the couch in the living room so he can watch a game. He won't let us eat there in front of the TV. And that is a gift.

Years ago, at the Museum of Fine Arts in Boston, I got to see Robert Therrien's gargantuan piece *Under the Table*. Given its absolutely gigantic scale, the viewer can walk under the dining table and even the chairs. This dinner table is at once a mundane, daily, domestic object and is at the same time overwhelming, intimidating, larger than life. I stood there in the museum and instantly related to this piece of art, to its surreal absurdity. To the ways that dinner tables can bring forth fantasy, fun, festivity and yet also invoke fear. It was at dinner tables with my dad that his presence was often enormous and where I often shrank, recoiled, and tried to hide.

The dinner table is iconic in art. There is Judy Chicago's *The Dinner Party*, which I saw when I was too little to appreciate and understand feminist revision. And there is also Bryan Geary's sculptural work of furniture titled *Rift* featuring a wooden table with cuts in it. The sides and backs of two chairs are inserted in those spaces with the chairs facing away from each other. It's evocative in terms of how we sit at tables to break bread together and yet so often find ourselves sitting in silence, just stuffing food in our faces, or at odds with each other and arguing, or tethered to our phones, venturing further and further from any hope of connected, communal space.

I think dinner tables shrink and expand in proportion to our losses, to our grief, to trauma, to whatever actually consumes us. See, before food made me sad, it often made me afraid. It made me anxious and worried, and it made me angry.

During the Martin Luther King Jr. holiday weekend in 1995, when Mark and I were newly dating, he came home with me to meet my parents. My mother's sixtieth birthday was approaching on January 24, and we decided to celebrate early. We had a lavish lobster dinner at home—a fine introduction for Mark, who had grown up in an Orthodox Jewish home, to delight in *treyf* with agnostic and atheist Jews. As we approached dessert, we brought out gifts for my mother to open.

My dad had asked me to do him a favor and shop for a gift for my mother that would be from the two of us. I went to the store located in the Cleveland Museum of Art, since it was always one of my mom's favorite places. There, I chose an unusual necklace of glass beads with colors bursting inside resembling the fancy candies I enjoyed in grade school given out by a woman in the neighborhood. The beads were stunning, and it seemed no one had such a necklace. This would surely be desirable to my free-spirited mother who resisted anything seemingly pedestrian. And it was fun to select an exquisitely crafted gift for her.

But when my mom opened her gift over dessert, the expression on her face revealed that this was not exactly the perfect present. My dad said, "What's wrong, Nimi? Don't you like it? Debbie and I thought it was just your style." And she replied, "Well, it's okay, but . . ." and before she could utter anything more, and rather than sing happy birthday, my dad shouted at her, "You cunt! You fucking ungrateful cunt!" I thought, "No, Dad, it's fine. I just got the wrong necklace. I made a poor choice. Don't be mad at Mom. It's her birthday."

My bulging green eyes shifted to Mark, who always compensated by eating more when he was uncomfortable and didn't want to talk. I guess his thought was "Keep shoveling it in, and eventually the other stuff will go away." Normally, I would have either talked back to one or both of them, yelled back, or gotten up from the table. This time, none of those options seemed workable. Mark was there, and we had only been dating for four and a half months. That's still the information-gathering stage in a relationship, where you're learning not just about your partner's personality but also about their inner circle of family and friends and what makes them tick. There were some things I couldn't bear to let Mark see, at least not that early on. And yet in that moment, I knew he had already seen too much. I wanted so desperately to run and hide, to magically erase everything that had just happened. Very late in the night, probably more like the wee hours of the morning, Mark and I were doing laundry in the basement, and as I went to hang something up on the clothesline, he touched my arm, looked at me, and told me he loved me. He showed me that he wanted to love me despite the plateful of shame that I'd never get rid of. The next morning, the day we were to return to Boston, my mom gave us a letter, addressed to both of us, apologizing for what we had witnessed and encouraging us to not let that ugliness find its way into our relationship. She didn't make excuses for my father, she said she was sorry if she played any role in what had happened, and she also made it clear that this was not exactly a one-time occurrence. It's those last two things that would remain the most confusing and sad.

That same year in the battering intervention program where I worked, I counseled a man who, when asked about his verbal abuse toward his partner, said that he repeatedly called her a bitch, a cunt, and a whore, but never stupid, because he admitted she wasn't stupid. Somehow in this linguistic construction, he affirmed his belief that she was indeed a bitch, a cunt, and a whore.

I realize I don't recall my father ever calling my mother stupid either, because she's not. She has a bachelor of arts from Michigan and a master of arts from Columbia and lots of street smarts and emotional intelligence, and she's an incredible artist. So stupid never quite fit. But according to my dad, my mom was a bitch, a cunt, and a whore—because he said so. He had called her a bitch plenty of times; at her sixtieth birthday party, he called her a cunt, and after they initially split up, he referred to her as a cock-sucking whore.

Every Tuesday night and Friday morning in counseling sessions with violent men, it was routine and almost mechanical to record clinical notes indicating men's callous accounts of calling their female partners all these god-awful names and then some—words like "cum dumpster" and "douche-bag" became new vocabulary. It's one thing to hear this stuff from men I had never lived with or loved or trusted, but it was entirely something else to hear it from the one man who had taught me how to ride a bicycle, who tested me on words to prepare for spelling bees, who took me in the shower with our bathing suits on so I could learn to shower, or who generously took me and any number of my friends to Sea World and Cedar Point.

Resisting violence in the context of intimacy means negotiating the rough, jagged edges of abuse with the tender, softer, smoother planes of love; the often irreconcilable tension and irreversible regret are lodged in the ambivalence of simultaneously wanting the abuse to stop and wanting the relationship to continue. Women like my mother and me who have stayed in abusive situations are merely conforming—maybe overly so—to rigid expectations of femininity. We did what good women were supposed to do. We forged and sustained a relationship. So when everyone keeps asking, "Why does she stay?" or "Why doesn't she just leave?" we aren't only diverting our attention away from more pressing questions such as "Why is her partner abusive?" and "Why does our society tolerate this?" but we are also suggesting that at a time of deepened vulnerability, the woman in question also deviates from all the ways she has been socialized.

No more. No longer do we have to endure dinners like that together. And no one died for this to happen. My father did not kill my mother and turn the gun on himself. The fact that my mind even works this way reminds me of an old, dear friend, a self-identified formerly battered woman, who once described to me what it was like to endure abuse from her professor husband. One day, they were out in their garden working in the flower beds, and he was hammering in posts, and with the hammer in his swinging arms, all she could think was how lucky she was that he was in a good mood, that they were having a relatively pleasant day. Abuse distorts our thinking. It pushes hypervigilance to its furthest edge. It makes us imagine and know that which should never be imaginable or knowable. The psychologist and researcher Rebecca Campbell says something similar about rape: "There really should be no space or a mechanism for understanding what this is."

The emotional, verbal, and financial abuse that permeated my parents' marriage for nearly thirty-two years did not lead to emergency room visits, shelters, or graveyards. Yet in absorbing the shock waves of their divorce in my early thirties and since then, something definitely died. Both the reality of our tiny family and the fantasies of what it might look like if affection and tenderness superseded cruelty most certainly died. So no more dinners together. Ever. Those had died.

The last time we ever sat in a restaurant together was at Blue Ginger in Wellesley, Massachusetts, on June 29, 2003, my wedding day with Mark. I came up with the idea that he and I would sit at our own table, partly to create an intimate setting and partly, more honestly, to avoid sitting with all our parents together and my parents' partners. We were trying to have tables of no more than six people, and his parents, my mom and Allan, my dad and Marla, and ourselves—plus a few chairs to seat the bodies of confusion and awkwardness and the silhouettes of abuse and the betrayal that brings—would be more than a table of twelve.

In his apartment alone after the divorce, my dad talked about wanting to invite Rob and Fiona for an extravagant dinner, since Rob had long been one of his closest friends. Fiona was a great cook. My dad had helped her put together a cookbook, and yet in return, I later learned from my mother that she had the chutzpah to refer to him as a beached whale. Perhaps elements of this were true, but it was also cruel. As a child, my dad was often a source of embarrassment. He was always the oldest father in my group of friends; he had me when he was forty-two. And he was fat and loud. He wasn't fat everywhere; he just had a Santa Claus–like belly, but I found it embarrassing as a young girl.

My dad was known for making a big scene in restaurants. Even before arriving at restaurants, he made a big production. He made reservations at multiple places so we'd have choices; he'd call and change the times, cancel some, forget to cancel others. Once there, the waitstaff usually never pleased him. Sometimes there was too much ice in the glass, sometimes not enough; sometimes the steak was too rare, sometimes it was overdone; sometimes they came to take our order too quickly so my dad felt rushed, other times they were too slow and he felt forgotten about. Sometimes he got friendly with the maître d' and got a great table, other times he insulted them for seating us near the kitchen or the bathroom; sometimes I said the wrong thing, other times my mom did. Or even more embarrassing to me were the times that he was critical of Mark at restaurants. I remember the time he got upset with how Mark buttered his bread, slathering butter on large slices rather than first ripping it and then buttering. The dinner table was contested space where humiliation and shame were acted out in the most public of ways.

When my dad was living at the nursing home, he was invited to his dear friend's ninetieth birthday at Oakwood Country Club. More than anything, he wanted to be there. But to go, he needed assistance. Lots of it. He needed transportation and an aide, and it was all much more expensive than I could afford. His friend wanted him to be able to attend, so he paid for it all. I didn't feel too guilty; he was a multimillionaire, and I was an adjunct professor at a university. But I felt bad for how my dad had to get there, that he needed a ride and an aide in order to be able to attend. Once at the party, he indulged in one of his favorite martinis and then later had an accident in his pants. When they called to tell me what happened, it struck me as very sad. And it seemed like a cruel joke that was played on him—the master of public taunting was then shamed publicly.

When I got my PhD in 2005, my dad wanted to take me out to celebrate with my three closest girlfriends from childhood and their husbands. This was in the very early days of when he was ill, when he was still living at home with the help of a walker and visiting nurses. He wanted to take us to Red, an incredible steakhouse in Beachwood. When I dream of a luscious steak or tater tots with crispy edges and fluffy insides, Red is the place that comes to mind. I remember wanting to eat there, wanting to be with my friends, wanting to celebrate this accomplishment that really meant more to my father than it did to me, and yet I canceled the reservation. I used the excuse that it all seemed like too much, that it wasn't necessary, that it would take a lot of energy to get there, that I wasn't feeling so great. It's really that I couldn't bear the idea of my dad doing anything to embarrass me in front of Renee, Betsy, and Erica.

Today, I live with the disappointment I am sure it created for my dad to not go, to not publicly celebrate this moment. We had a long history of celebrating my academic milestones over food and drink; when I earned a great report card in elementary school, middle school, and high school, my parents took me to special places for dinner. Red was my last chance for this type of celebration, and I blew it. Well, I know he had done the stuff to blow it, to make me feel I needed to cancel our dinner. But still, even today, the fact that that evening never happened makes me feel guilty, sad, and ashamed. So if you were to ask me, "If you could have dinner with anyone in the world, who would it be?" without hesitation, I'd say, "My dad." It may be foolish, I know. I think I just want one more shot, one more chance to try to get it right.

I love having the chance to eat with my mom, yet I have to admit that something is missing when we get together. The something, of course, is my dad—the imprint of what a family dinner is or should be. The table looks and feels too small to be real, like two women trying to eat at a table out of a dollhouse. When people leave or die, the dinner table shrinks. The holiday tables shrivel up. Sometimes new people come and sit in the empty chairs. They fill in. We reinvent the rituals. I wonder how many different iterations of dinner tables I will live through.

After my dad died, the social worker at the nursing home sent me his belongings in a cardboard box. It was too expensive to ship everything, and all I wanted was his Nikon camera and the paintings and photographs he had on the walls in his room. Many of the things I had most wanted and cared about were already in my home from when I had moved him to the nursing home in the first place. And I wanted to minimize how much of that sad nursing home to send to my new home anyway, how much to let it enter and penetrate my new space. He had just died, and I wasn't in good shape to decide what to keep and what to let go of over the telephone while talking with the social worker.

As it turns out, they could not have packed it more sloppily, and so some pictures were water damaged, soiled, and crushed. It was hard to believe that the belongings of this man, with such a huge personality, were jammed into one cardboard box, but if you have ever been to a nursing home, it makes sense in the grossest way. Underneath the veneer of bureaucratic order and record keeping and charts is whopping disorder, just a colossal mess. Everything is just thrown together in the most senseless way. Packages of Depends are stuffed next to family albums and wedding photos, and photos of children framed in glass and silver are standing next to plastic urinals on rolling tables. Favorite heirlooms are stashed beside Kleenex boxes and sanitary wipes; empty plastic bedpans sit atop important handmade quilts. It's all a mad, fierce juxtaposition.

My mom once told me the story of when her mother died and she went to pick up her belongings at the nursing home. She had already told the staff she was leaving the television and the walker so another resident could benefit from those items. The only big thing my mother wanted was a special wrought-iron lamp that she still uses to read by. All I wanted was my dad's camera. Two daughters just wanting to capture that same light through which their own parents saw the world. Lamps and cameras; lightness and darkness; clarity and obscurity; reflections thrown all around the room.

My mom said that when she arrived at the nursing home to pick up the stuff, she waited in the long hall, and a man appeared with a dolly, and on it were the contents of my grandmother's room, of all that remained of her life up to that point. And on the dolly was a large black plastic garbage bag filled with all the tchotchkes that had been in her room—once-treasured belongings she had lovingly gathered on trips with my grandfather. And my grandmother was someone who was fastidious, who took the greatest pride in how she presented herself to the world and in how she entertained at home, with meticulous attention paid to every detail. And as my mom stood there, rummaging through the bag, everything she had come for suddenly lost its appeal and its importance. In the garbage bag, what was once beautiful looked trashy. And so she said to the people working there, "Please take from this what you want and feel free to dispose of the rest."

What we come for can't be gotten in the bags and on the dollies, and what's sent to us in the mail isn't what we yearn to have and to hold. Perhaps these nursing homes do us a favor. In making an unappetizing, grotesque mess of it all, we come to want the stuff less, and maybe this helps us need it less.

Given all this disarray, it's no surprise then that at the bottom of the box that was sent to me, I found the contents of the top drawer of my dad's nightstand. The social worker put that stuff in a quart-sized Ziploc bag, and in the area where people would normally write "chicken breast" or "blackened tilapia," maybe with the date so they know how long to keep it in the refrigerator or freezer, she wrote, "Cohan wallet."

Inside the plastic bag was a tired black leather wallet with fifteen different cards and pictures in the following order: a driver's license issued on July 25, 2003, less than a month after Mark and I got married and exactly seventeen months to the day before all hell would break loose in our lives and my dad would fracture his hip at Cleveland Hopkins International Airport; a social security card; his Medicare health insurance card; his GE Long-Term Care Insurance policyholder card; an AARP card; two AARP Health Options cards, one in paper and one in plastic; a card indicating the stent in his heart that was implanted in 2002; another version of that same card also indicating the location of the stent; a Golden Buckeye Card issued by the Ohio Department of Aging; two AAA Bail Bond certificate cards, one that was somehow stuck to a picture of me from my sophomore year of college, which happened to be one of my parents' favorite photos of me; my college yearbook photo with a faded inscription on the back that read, "I love you, Dad; thanks for everything. You're the best"; and two photos of me with Mark in Austin, Texas, in 1996, when our love was new, two months before we moved in together for what would be the first time. Before the breakup and the makeup and the trying again and the marriage and the divorce.

Seeing the contents of my dad's wallet after his death was a little like finding that chicken or tilapia that had been stored in the back of the freezer for years, forgotten and way past its freshness. Everything in the wallet had long expired, even my marriage to Mark. All the cards my dad had in there were about managing his aging and increasingly poor health. I realized that the only things that had any life left in them were the photos of me, and that made me even sadder; I had been too much of my dad's life, and here was more evidence of that. It all reminded me of a Father's Day card I had sent to him the summer after I graduated from college in which I wrote, "Please know that I want more than anything to see you doing things that make you happy. You said to me while I was home that you feel like you have spent your life living it for others. Daddy—don't live your life for me, and please don't live my life for me."

Besides the wallet that I found in the plastic bag, there was also a white envelope marked "James Cohan" that had a little list written on it of the cash he spent on food for the last two months of his life—his last meals. Residents are allowed very little personal spending money in these homes, and so all he started with in June 2012 was fifty dollars, an amount he would have previously blown, easily, on a nice lunch years before. Nineteen dollars was spent on pizza; I assume that some staff members indulged in that with him and that he treated them without even consenting to it. The only date that was recorded was one dollar that was spent on a cheese-burger on June 24, 2012, about seven weeks before he died. I am not sure where anyone found him a burger for a dollar, but I know for sure it was like none of the burgers he used to eat years and years before. I have never been so depressed about a hamburger. Then I noticed on this little accounting of expenses that $8.62 was added and then another $4.66, totaling $43.28 at the time of his death. The social worker enclosed the bills and the coins in that envelope.

My once brilliant, successful, financially secure father died, and all I got was this lousy $43.28. It sounds crass, but my bitterness stems from the fact that I know for sure that he intended to leave me with so much more when he died. He had wanted there to be enough money to pay off my graduate student loans and to have money for some exotic travel. But he had no way of knowing how sick he would be for so long and how being on Medicaid would wipe it all out. The truth is, of course, that he did leave me with so much more than money, but for him, being able to leave me with something big materially would have made him prouder, would have confirmed that he had accomplished what it meant to him to be a good father who provided well for his daughter. So I was never angry that there was so little money left at the end. Rather, I was in disbelief that this is what a life can amount to, and I felt frustrated for him. I have also never found it as revolting to receive money as I did then. I can't even remember what I did with it, only that I shoved it in my wallet with tremendous shame, sadness, and horror, like I had just stolen something but couldn't give it back, and vowed to spend it on anything but food.

7

The Kaleidoscope

There is a crack, a crack in everything
That's how the light gets in.
—Leonard Cohen, "Anthem"

Red Suitcase

On one of my visits to the nursing home, I found that they had just moved my dad to a new room again. Next to the closet stood the red suitcase—that same fucking red suitcase that accompanied my father to every room in every nursing home in which he had been housed for almost eight years. The suitcase that went everywhere with him somehow took him nowhere. I wanted to somehow shred the suitcase into a million little pieces, or burn it, or throw it out the window, but definitely kill it. Let's face it: he was never going to go anywhere with it. I was so angry at the suitcase. I felt like it betrayed my father and me.

Suitcases are supposed to take us places. Exotic places. Places where fantasies can take flight. Upon packing one, we neatly fold our plans and layer our dreams, outfit by outfit, shoe by shoe. I pack, or more accurately overpack, my suitcases for trips with a sort of nervous excitement and longing.

I hope I will arrive at my destination, able to travel in a way that shifts time and space, at least temporarily. That lets me experience my body and myself in new ways, in new depths. Suitcases hold promise.

My dad's red suitcase contained only knotted-up dreams. On Christmas Day 2004, my dad was supposed to meet Mark and me at Cleveland Hopkins International Airport so we could all fly together to Delray Beach for a vacation. Mark and I flew in from Boston, and as we landed in Cleveland, I was paged on the airplane. We learned that my father had fallen on ice getting out of a limousine at United Airlines departures and never made it to the gate. So that red suitcase was first rushed to the emergency room at Fairview Park Hospital, then to Hillcrest Hospital, then to Stein Nursing Home, then to Bloomberg Park, then briefly home, then to the Avon Commons Nursing Home, and then the Regal Care Nursing Home.

That red suitcase was supposed to go to Palm Beach International Airport and then on to a five-star luxury hotel to be whisked away by a bellhop who would take it to the highest floor overlooking the beach. Instead, my dad lived on the first floor of a nursing home—he was not a wanderer with his dementia, so the first floor was safe. He couldn't even get out of a wheelchair by himself, so there was no risk that he would bolt through the doors.

We were all supposed to order those umbrella drinks out by the pool. At the nursing home, the staff ordered my dad thickened liquids in Styrofoam cups so he could drink without choking. Inside the suitcase were my dad's swimming trunks; in the years before he fell, he rarely swam, but when he did, he was still really good. One never loses their form—well, at least their swimming form. He had been captain of the Syracuse swim team decades earlier. But at the home, in order to prevent him from swimming in his own shit and urine, the nursing aides dressed him in Depends.

How could I be this mad *at a suitcase*? I mean, who's crazy here? Still, when I walk into the luggage section at TJ Maxx, I can't bear the look of the red suitcases. In fact, when I went to visit my friend Lisa in the Netherlands, we were at the baggage carousel at the airport, waiting for my luggage. When my bag was nowhere to be found, she said, "You know, Deb, this is why I got my printed suitcase. It's easier to find in the crowd. You really should consider a bright bag, maybe red or something rather than the same huge black one that everyone has. And you've always loved red." I wanted to scream, "Fuck, no, I will *never* carry a red suitcase. I mean, yeah, red is my favorite color, but not for suitcases. They should not even *make* red suitcases. Red suitcases don't get you where you want to go. They fuck with your plans, your dreams, your life."

One afternoon after that trip, I was back in Boston, drinking a steaming mug of chai, studying the living room in a "my days are numbered here" sort of stare. In particular, I fixated on the red upholstered, upright, yet somehow comfortable chair, the one that had been red-and-white-polka-dotted velvet in the sunken living room on Morley Road when I was a little girl. But when my parents divorced, they split up the pair of chairs; my mom took one and upholstered it in velvet, the color of a ripe eggplant. My father took his chair and made it bright red. I always secretly liked my dad's better. My mother's struck me as the one to read a book in and get sleepy; my dad's chair had verve and gusto. After I moved him into the nursing home for good, I sent his furniture to our house in Boston. My dad and I shared a love for the same color palette, so everything worked together; one could not tell what had been his and what was Mark's and mine. I contemplated moving again—this time alone—to a place still unknown to me as I renavigated the national academic job market. I had not yet received my job offer from the University of South Carolina. So I wondered, "Where would this red chair go next? Would it be to a warmer climate, a smaller city, a less manic one, a place where I know at least one other person? Who would sit in the chair one day? Would it be someone I would grow to love, someone who would move from the chair to the couch to cozy up with me?" Unlike the red suitcase, the chair has open sides and openness under the back and right above the plush, full seat; in the spaces, there's breathing room. There's room for dreams to enter and float through and a place for them to perch on the seat and the armrests. I sat on this chair when I was as young as three years old, when my patent leather Mary Janes couldn't reach the floor, not even the end of the seat. I thought to myself, "What's next in store for this chair? What's next in store for me?"

I became obsessed with thinking about what life would look like in six months, twelve months, and beyond. Then I did reverse math, thinking about what I was doing twelve months prior, what I planned for my life that had happened and what I had no idea about that still would be in store for me. A year earlier, when Mark and I traveled to Oahu to celebrate his fiftieth birthday and my fortieth birthday, I never imagined that I would ever look at the red chair and wonder that it would be anywhere but firmly grounded in our living room. I had not yet met divorce attorneys and changed beneficiaries or made lists with lines down the middle of "Mark's Stuff" and "Deb's Stuff," and I had not yet thought about the identity shift involved in checking the divorced box when I updated the forms at my annual physical.

I wonder about the things we carry with us, the things we move around, the character they take on, and the energy they absorb in new environments. I have always been fascinated by our relationships with things, not in a materialistic way so much as a sociologically curious way. In fact, I cannot shop online, as I need and want to touch everything. It's why my mother claims to detest shopping with me. The part of me interested in Buddhism understands it is best not to cling, to not be attached. Ironically, or maybe not, I bought a lot of Buddhist books to think through that sense of impermanence. Looking back, I could have saved a whole lot of cash. All it really takes is a parent with dementia to realize this crucial life lesson. Here it is—my dad took a lot of time and money to accumulate all he had. He spent time consulting with people, ordering stuff, making calls, buying, and returning. I do this too. "Is it worth it?" I often think. But then again, I like being able to serve salad in a bowl that my father found and loved. I like using the same pen he used to craft copy for advertising campaigns, as it makes me feel like I can be more creative and inspired, that my own way of ordering words will be sharper. His room in the nursing home had the equivalent of cheap college dorm furniture for dressers and nightstands, and of course there was the hospital bed, the wheelchair, a dusty rose recliner, and some mementos of a past life—some framed pictures and photographs. Fake plants, plastic reachers, and a commode replaced the objects he once enjoyed in his home. Even my dad's Paul Jenkins framed print, drenched with bright colors, looked dreary and dismal and downright out of place in the nursing home. It was too beautiful, too bright for that place. And so was my dad. This man, whose presence was larger than life, did not belong in that constantly shrinking place. I wondered if I would want this piece of art for my home when he died. Who in their right mind would turn down a Paul Jenkins painting or leave it in the dumpster behind a nursing home? But who could take it, knowing where it has been? We are our stuff. Our stuff is us. We are not our stuff. Our stuff is not us. We are our plans. Our plans are us. We are not our plans. Our plans are not us.

Black Datebooks

My dad always made intricate plans for travel. He bought all the new Fodor's and Frommer's travel books, the Zagat guides, and the books featuring the best, smallest, most historic boutique hotels in the world. When my dad finally had to give up his apartment, I found elaborate travel plans he dreamed up but never executed—villas he considered renting in Greece and Italy, listings of the best restaurants to try and galleries to explore. I am not sure what was more impossibly sad to find when I closed up my dad's apartment for good—these extensive travel plans that were written about but not taken or my dad's black datebooks from the years since he and my mom had divorced, detailing every lunch, meeting, symphony concert, date with a woman, therapy session, medical appointment, haircut, and theater production he attended, punctuated with "See Debbie and Mark in Boston" or "Debbie and Mark arrive" or "Order roses for Debbie." I was an observer to the roads he traveled, the detours he was subjected to, and the journeys never taken.

I kept my dad's datebooks. I kept them in a fit of sorrow and of really not knowing what to keep and throw away. I kept them with the hope that I would eventually write about my relationship with him, what it deprived me of and what it gave me, and because I guess I intuited that one day I would be comforted by finding the datebooks, which I could open up to the current day and see exactly what my dad was doing that same day, however many years earlier. Sometimes I still peek through those calendars—it is January 22; I wonder what my dad was doing on this day in 2000 or 2003. My curiosity has become an obsession. Sometimes I play games with them, searching for patterns or even considering his handwriting and when it changed and how this relates to his deterioration and when he fell. I have always had an interest in details and habits others might regard as trivial and mundane. For example, I want to know the first thing someone does when they get news their loved one dies. I want to know what my friend wore on her first date. I want to know where they ate. I am interested in what people do when they first wake up in the morning, how others get motivated to write and the rituals they use to get themselves into the act of doing anything creative, what people think of when they are having sex, and what they do after sex.

I told my mother I kept the datebooks. "Debbie, what would you want with them?" she asked half inquisitively, half judgingly. I couldn't bear to throw out the records of my dad's days, no matter if they appeared lonelier and sadder as he got sicker and sicker. Discarding his days felt to me, in essence, like trashing his life, and I was not prepared to do this. I know that when I even temporarily misplace my datebook, I feel disoriented, like I lost my life, like the road map of where I have been and where I am going is obliterated. The datebooks became a way for me to connect the dots of my dad's life and eventually to connect the dots of my own life back to his.

The last time my dad was able to write in and maintain these datebooks was in the spring of 2006, and by then, much less was written in them. He was living in his apartment with around-the-clock care, and there was not much to fill those blank white squares, the ones I treasure when I buy my new calendars each year, thinking about how I will fill my days and weeks and months. Before each new year, I approach the calendar as a meticulous calligrapher, using only pencil, wanting to write each appointment and task with order and care. By late January, my datebook resembles a suitcase I have packed for a trip—overstuffed with activities and bursting with no space to breathe. There are pen marks, and high-lights, and things scratched out, and I at once berate myself for another year of not being neat and organized and therefore not good enough, and at the same time I am happy to be more carefree, to realize that real life does not happen the way I imagine it to be when I start my datebook on January 1.

My dad's datebooks help me understand how ordinary life is, and his travel plans help me understand how often we try to escape what feels so ordinary. I realize the way I live my life is both as well. I often feel bogged down by the mundane parts of life: the laundry, the grocery shopping, the constant errands—what my wise, compassionate friend Nancy aptly and more kindly calls "life maintenance."

In elementary school, I was so excited about planning a fun weekend with my parents that I even wrote a list on Friday and titled it "Our Big Weekend." I look back on that as a symbol of both my need to plan and my somewhat larger need to be sure fun could always happen. As an adult, there are places in my life where I strive for profound order: in my relentless list making, my work spaces and living spaces, and my lifelong attraction to minimalist design. Sometimes in the height of a creative work project, I obviously have to abandon some of that. But also as an adult, I crave spontaneity and playfulness and try to be sure that even if structure or semistructure is a necessary overlay, that there is also time and flexibility for a detour to allow for some surprise or change that can wind up being more fun in the end. I think the more the world feels unpredictable and scary, the more we look for minutiae in our lives to control. Simultaneously, the more the world gets so formulaic and boringly predictable, the more I want spontaneity and real rather than prefab and manufactured joy.

Closer to when I moved my dad into the nursing home, seeing the datebooks generated an urgent nagging, like someone screaming from inside me, "When are you going to live your life? When are you going to actualize the big life you *say* you want? Be sure to do these things and don't just talk about them." And I also remember thinking, with the things I do get to do—even the more mundane stuff like the car repairs and the grocery store and the coffee dates with friends—that I wanted to do them more joyfully and wholeheartedly. When watching a parent so near death, you can't help but gently whisper to yourself—or in my case, hurriedly, harshly, and obnoxiously scream at yourself—"Grow, flourish, do it. Do something. Anything. Just make it happen *now*."

The longer I have lived with these datebooks, however, I find that stumbling upon them in the middle of the night becomes tremendously reassuring—a reminder of how life is bigger than we are, how people have struggled with the same tasks and plans and questions and hopes and dreams for centuries. The datebooks slow me down in a good way. It is akin to when I wash dishes—sometimes I have a voice inside me screaming, "Come on; hurry up, already. We have better things to be doing with our time." And then at other moments, I feel connected to Nonnie, my maternal grandmother, the one who was a dear friend to me, who often baked cookies at 2:00 a.m. as I have done, and I think of her in her tiny little kitchen on Van Aken Boulevard, and then I wonder about her mother, my great-grandmother, the one I never met but was named after. I am flooded with imaginings of worlds of women, ones I know and ones I have never met, washing dishes and scrubbing away worries and imperfections, searching for reflections and beauty and long-held dreams in dirty dishwater and clean plates.

Years back, a boyfriend I was truly crazy about sent me an email in which he revealed this about himself:

One of the things I've come to know about myself is how much I enjoy looking forward to things. I may be the only person in the world except maybe a travel agent who enjoys PLANNING a trip more than actually taking it. The planning is always perfect. What actually happens is filled with delays, bad food, annoying people, etc. I think it also fills my need for order; in the planning stages, I can arrange things to happen in an orderly, efficient, and logical manner. (Maybe I should have joined the military.) Life, of course, is never like that.

He wrote that to me as we planned a visit for me to go out to see him. I now understand this to be an awfully big red flag, one that I was not able to see waving as brightly then. I was attracted to him and even had moments of thinking that his reluctance to travel seemed endearing, that perhaps one day, he would like the trip more than the plans if only with me. I also felt sad for him. His confession was incredibly honest but usually not articulated by most people. I intuited that some aspect of all this planning had to be about self-protection. And I wanted to completely disagree with him, but I couldn't. I want to be the person who plans something—or maybe skips planning something altogether—and has the best time anyway. I wanted to take the position that anything could be good enough if only we could tame our expectations long enough. But his message forced me to realize how much I do that too—how much I plan and am then often disappointed. Our minds can conjure up anything and can take us on fabulous journeys, but in the real, lived moment, we are left with the demands of life, other people's stuff, and our often-unmet expectations and desires.

Reading that email, I immediately thought of my father, the ultimate maven on could haves, would haves, and should haves on every trip we took. Though there were many times I thought I wanted nothing more than to plan things with this boyfriend or make things happen with him, what I realized soon enough was that for me to be happy in a relationship, the present would have to look as sweet as any plans. The present would have to be the real litmus test for a possible relationship. Poring over my dad's datebooks and rereading my old boyfriend's message and then meditating on how I imagine my life will be in the future makes me realize more and more that life is pretty ordinary. If we're lucky, the extraordinary moments happen in the context of the ordinary stuff, like Nancy's gentle approach has helped me to see. The extraordinary moments happen most easily when we abandon our plans and our lists, both the ones in our datebooks and the ones we so carefully lay out on paper for travel "someday."

My father's elaborate travel plans that never happened worried me for the fact that they conveyed a spectator's life. My dad and that boyfriend of mine had something in common: they were both addicted to the notion of perfect plans. I think back on every man I have loved or lived with or had a mad crush on before Mike, and addiction is a running theme. Not only was my dad addicted to perfecting plans, making reservations, canceling them, and reinstating them; he was also addicted to food and lavish restaurants and rage. There was the college boyfriend who moved to Texas to be with me in graduate school who was addicted to the bottle. There was the friend from college who became more than a friend on multiple occasions who was like George Clooney's character in that movie *Up in the Air*, a man enmeshed in a complex love triangle with ambition and solitude. And there were all the men I dated who were addicted to exercise, pornography, work, and other women. Finally there was Mark, the man who for years I loved the most and lived with the longest, who was addicted to the television.

Blue Light

I often felt the same way about the television in my marriage to Mark as I felt about my dad's red suitcase in the nursing home. It just sat there and did nothing for us. It was always there, with the promise of pulling us into other worlds. But in reality, it was a big empty box that really took us nowhere except far from each other. It was a box of stagnation. Like the suitcase, it betrayed us. I have come to understand loneliness and deferred dreams in two ways: as a red suitcase and as blue light—the blue light that emanates from the television.

I'll be blunt: I hate TV. Every few years, there are shows I like to watch. As a kid, I watched *The Brady Bunch*, *Eight Is Enough*, *One Day at a Time*, or *Family Ties*. As a teenager, I loved *Thirtysomething*, and in my twenties, I watched *Once and Again*, the 1990s version of *Thirtysomething*. In 2005 or so, I started watching HGTV because I adore interior design and reconceptualizing space, and in 2010, I started to like the show *Modern Family*. Other than this, I rarely watch television. Essentially, I use it as a tool for watching movies. I brought this up in therapy, and the therapist suggested that Mark get headphones so that I would not have to hear the television. Finally, he did, and as was to be expected, this brought forth other problems and created deeper chasms.

People ask me the moment I knew I wanted the divorce. For some people in troubled marriages, maybe there is a crystal-clear moment—a moment so outrageous you know you can't continue to live like that anymore or you will go insane. Or there is a "last straw" moment. Or maybe there's a moment that suggests that the pain of staying in the marriage exceeds the pain of leaving. I also think there could be the nonmoment moment, the moment when nothing particularly horrible has happened that is different but one that comes with a sense that everything could continue this way forever if you don't stop it, which becomes overwhelming.

My friend Hope, who has been divorced twice, leaned in to me at dinner one night and asked, "What was the moment you knew? Don't you think there is just that one defining moment?" She told me hers: apparently, it was when her first ex-husband said something rude and dismissive to her mother on Christmas Eve, and she had had enough of his nastiness toward everyone around her. She even recalled that her mother did not think it was so terrible, yet for Hope, that moment was the deal breaker. My other friend admitted that when things got terrible between her and her spouse, she started to wish her husband would just get hit by a bus. While that seems cruel, I understood the desperate sense of being stuck and just wishing for a way out.

I explained my "moment" to Hope over dinner: "This is going to sound crazy, but I was sick of coming home late from teaching or whatever I was doing and seeing our house from the intersection a little ways away, with the neighborhood completely dark and the only light that was visible being the flickering blue light of the television in our living room." I felt like I was coming home to a dark cave. This was a man who had majored in physical education but who was more content watching sports on TV. He also watched as much TV a day as is recommended for sleep every night. I began to hope for a partner vividly and vibrantly engaged with his life and our life. The real lightness I longed for was not available in our home, nor did I experience it in my childhood home; it would take years and a new partner to access that certain lightness of being.

For better and for worse, Mark never did remind me of my father. He was never as mean yet also never as generous. I grew weary of Mark's obsessive coupon collecting, the fact that he would buy things he didn't want or need just because they were on sale or they were buy one, get one free and then keep them, believing maybe one day he would use these things. He also stored empty boxes for small appliances in the basement because he hated throwing anything out, and he was so self-denying that in turn, I was also denied and stifled. Mark was never cruel to strangers like my father felt entitled to be, yet he was also never as wildly complimentary to me either. But as Mark started to watch an increasing amount of television, he began to resemble my father, and at that point, our marriage started to look like my parents'. The meanest thing I ever said to my mother, that I wish I could take back, was when I told her I wanted a divorce and explained that I just didn't want to wait twenty-four more years like she did to finally change my life. I was forty when I made this decision. She was sixty-four. It sounded like I was judging her for wasting her life with my dad.

My dad watched a crazy amount of television. On the one hand, it seemed like no big deal, like it was an extension of his work; he worked in advertising, and he studied commercials. On the other hand, it was an enormous deal. It kept him in a constant state of loneliness, driving a wedge between him and my mother and taking him away from real-life experiences with other hobbies and friends. My mother was in a constant chase for stimulation in her own way, always hurtling to the next activity—retreating to her studio to paint, leaving the house to gather apples in the fall, exploring a new museum or a recently renovated part of downtown, or taking long walks in the Metro Parks. She would have loved for my father to go on at least some of these adventures. My father would have been happy if my mother sat down beside him to watch television, even a few weekly programs. It was clear that neither would ever happen. This impasse made Sundays a day I learned to detest, for this was the main day on which this chasm deepened.

In my mother, I had a powerful role model for retaining a strong sense of individuality in the context of a relationship. And as Mark's behavior mirrored my dad's more and more, I perfected this pulling away that she taught me. The legacy she gave me has provided some comfort, the idea that "two people need not be connected at the hip," a phrase she always used to show me that some independence in a relationship is crucial for retaining a sense of one's own interests. The problem is that I had never learned to balance this and existed in a relationship with Mark that cradled independence more than anything else. There were too many times I wrote cards to Mark for birthdays, anniversaries, and Valentine's Day in which I wished for us more joy and passion, two of the seven blessings we chose for ourselves at our wedding, as dimensions to nurture in our marriage.

My mother helped me learn at a very early age, in museums and in her basement studio, that light affects how we see color, that in turn color changes how we see light, and that light alters space. What I have grown to understand myself is that light, or the nature and absence of it, and color, or the nature and absence of it, saturate our memories and our abilities to see and also shape and sometimes distort our abilities to relate to ourselves and to be in relationships. Through how we craft the spaces we inhabit and the plans we concoct, our lives can become more narrow and more rigidly defined, or we can choose to breathfully and mindfully expand. I understand better now that place is imbued with meaning, that our perceptions of constraint and expanse are shaped by a complex prism—by a kaleidoscopic physical and emotional blend of color and light. I know—because the red suitcase, the black datebooks, and the blue light told me so.

8

Medical Records

Ten milligrams of Ambien for sleep.

Twenty milligrams of Glucotrol to regulate the diabetes.

Five hundred milligrams of Amoxicillin for god-knows-what infection from god-knows-what bacteria in the nursing home.

Thirty milligrams of Actos to control blood sugar. Wait, wasn't the Glucotrol for that?

Five hundred milligrams of Glucophage to control blood sugar, two tablets, two times a day. Weren't the Actos and the Glucotrol for that?

One hundred twenty-five milligrams of Mysoline for essential tremors of the hands.

Eighty milligrams of Diovan to control high blood pressure and heart failure.

Thirty milligrams of Imdur for angina.

Twenty milligrams of Nadolol for more of the angina. Was the Imdur not working well enough?

A drop in each eye at bedtime of Xalatan, to treat glaucoma.

Twenty-five milligrams, twice a day, of Aldactone to treat fluid retention.

Ten milligrams of Lipitor for cholesterol.

Two capsules, .4 milligrams each, of Flomax to help ease urination for an enlarged prostate.

Twenty milligrams of Demadex, twice a day, a diuretic used to treat edema. But wasn't the Aldactone for that?

Twenty milligrams of Paxil for depression. Fuck, who wouldn't be depressed?

Thirty milligrams of Prevacid for gastroesophageal reflux disease.

Two milligrams of Loperamide for diarrhea.

Sixty milligrams of Allegra for sneezing and allergies.

Six hundred milligrams of Humibid for cough and congestion.

Two hundred milligrams of Tessalon, also for cough.

And a Centrum Silver multivitamin, some glucosamine/ chondroitin, and an aspirin for good measure.

On a Visa bill from July 2005, my father paid $1,280 just to the pharmacy. I see now how he was mortgaging his finances for health he would never enjoy, a body he would never use, and a life that turned into a maddening combination of crushed powders, tablets with gelatin coatings, and liquids. One extra little something, slipped into this whole mess, would be untraceable.

Years ago, I came home from a solo trip to Cleveland and said to Mark, very matter-of-factly, "What if next time I go, I just poison my dad? You know, get some pills and help him die sooner, without all this pain." Looking at me a bit horrified, he said, "But, Deb, you can't, you'll be caught." Mark was so rule bound, so careful, so cautious. "But who would ever know?" I pressed on. "Deb, come on, they have ways of figuring this out," Mark replied, increasingly impatient with me. With a snippy tone, I snapped back, "Well, if your parents ever get this ill and you have to deal with this kind of shit, I bet you will want to help them end it. And fast."

Oh, trust me, before I had fantasies of helping my dad die faster and with greater ease, I was obsessed with everyone knowing everything possible just to keep him alive. At some point in caring for my dad long distance, I thought it would be best to make an emergency list for the nursing aides to have on the refrigerator at his apartment. I proceeded, in my typical obsessive-compulsive fashion, to distribute copies to everyone I could—his doctors, Mark, and even my mother. I figured that if anyone should call to ask any questions, we all needed to have the correct information documented. I wrote it as my father, in the first person:

The following medical conditions are part of my past and present medical history:
1. Heart attack (2001) and congestive heart failure; still in need of cardiac catheterization as of 12/04; two cardiac stents in place since 2001
2. Diabetes, Type II
3. Kidney stones, history of these since 1966; one stent in place from fall 2004 that will be removed
4. Aortic aneurysm, surgery occurred in 1987

5. Broken hip, 12/25/04, surgery included pins and screws to repair but not to replace
6. Sleep apnea
7. Essential tremors of the hands
8. Neuropathy
9. Edema in legs
10. Arthritis in hands
11. Partial in mouth
12. Gastrointestinal distress; diverticulitis in 1990s; chronic diarrhea

Caregiving amplified all that was already so unpredictable and in so doing also intensified all the ways I tend toward hyperresponsibility and hyperresponsiveness. Always one to keep files on anything and everything, to write reminder Post-its and multiple to-do lists, I even drove around in the car for more than a year with the file of my dad's living will, cremation arrangements, and payment forms. I never wanted to be caught somewhere unprepared, unable to answer someone's questions on my dad's behalf. Looking back, I think it was hypervigilance learned through abuse, cultivated in womanhood, and perfected through caregiving.

I understand where I got the tendency to document and record everything and to question authority. When I moved my father to the nursing home, I found a long letter he had written to his cardiologist in 2002, before he fell and his whole life toppled over, in which he expressed his worry and fear about the cocktail of drugs he was ingesting and the side effects they were producing. He went through the litany of medicines this doctor had prescribed and described every side effect in detail—the fatigue, decreased sex drive, dizziness, muscle aches, runny nose, swollen legs, purple and red spots on his skin, cold hands and feet, diarrhea, low blood pressure, trouble sleeping, and urinary problems. And with his characteristic acerbic wit, he wrote,

> Actos offers—at no additional charge—hypoglycemia, muscle aches, swelling, shortness of breath, and weight gain. Guess who's suffering from those . . . Glucotrol is a wonderful medication if you're looking to acquire diarrhea, dizziness, drowsiness, and tremors. I wasn't looking for them, but I got them. So what is happening? Why am I taking medications with so many harmful side effects and from which I am now suffering? Why am I taking so many medications? Why aren't tests being performed? Why can't I take a minimum of medication? I thought medicines were supposed to be therapeutic, not poisonous.

It's my dad's desperate, relentless, yet reasonable worries and fears so evident in these questions to his doctor that weigh on me now.

In the notes that the home health aide took when she cared for my dad in 2005, she wrote, "SOB." I thought it strange that the aides would be so blatant in calling patients "sons of bitches." My dad was one, technically speaking. His mother—my grandmother—was a bitch on wheels. But still, in *medical* files? It seemed so inappropriate. So I Googled it; it turns out that SOB also stands for "shortness of breath." In my family, we all had it, this shortness of breath. About this very same time, I was diagnosed with multiple upper respiratory infections and reactive airways—not surprising given that I was literally holding my breath for years managing all this caregiving.

The medical notes from February 22, 2005, state that my dad was angry at being awakened to take medicine. The aide quoted him saying, "I don't want pills at six a.m. I don't want to be woken up for any damn pills. You can take the pills and shove them." My mom always claimed that when she was around and had to deal with my dad being sick, he simultaneously wanted the doctors' attention and advice and also resented them, a man who both wanted a stash of medicine and didn't want to rely on it, a man who wanted it all his way.

And it's no wonder he was cranky, since things in my father's life were quickly being replaced. He once had a black leather Stressless chair in the living room. In 2005, the home health agency ordered him a special padded transfer chair, a shower chair, and a safety rail. He had been riding a red Giant bicycle and driving a Toyota Avalon, both of which were traded in for a motorized wheelchair. And of course, he had a wife, my mother, who got replaced by a short string of relatively unreliable girlfriends, the ones who could be counted on to spend a lot of my dad's money with him, who were right there to accompany him on lavish trips, but who disappeared when his health turned for the worse. The last one thought it would be cool to bring my diabetic father a huge Starbucks caramel Frappuccino in the hospital when he broke his hip and then vanished from his life when it became clear that he wasn't recovering well.

Earlier, there was Rachel, the girlfriend who called me in 2000, a year after my parents had gotten divorced, to say that my dad had sent her an email in which he claimed to be "tired of the misery" and in which he couldn't believe he had been married for thirty-two years and his life had turned out this way. Apparently she tried calling him in the morning and early afternoon, very concerned after reading his emails, and couldn't get through to him. So she called the police, the manager of the building let them in, and my dad was taken to a psychiatric emergency facility where he was hospitalized for "depression with suicidal ideation" and admitted against his will. I called my dad's attorney and his doctor, both of whom reinforced the message to me that he was lonely, he wanted his comfortable life back, and I was the only one left that he had in the world.

We've all heard that language about how in illness and disability, it can feel like our body has betrayed us. I'm not sure that is what happened to my father though. I am not sure he ever befriended his body in the first place or had a real, genuine, intimate relationship with his body for it to have actually betrayed him. When my dad talked about his body, all I heard about was pain. This was true even when he was generally okay as well as when he was sick. And he always yearned to be thinner, never doing much about it except trying fad diets. I don't think he liked his body much. I sometimes wonder what would have happened had I grown up with a more embodied father—a father more truly in and of and with and for his own body. Celebrating what the body is capable of doing, not just what's done to it, knowing it, maybe even trusting it, as a site and source of pleasure, not just a location of pain. I wonder what this would have done for me as a girl coming into my sense of my body or as a woman now in my late forties thinking about my own frailties and strengths.

When I packed up my dad's apartment and he was fully moved into the nursing home, I also had to close his safe deposit box at the bank. In it, I discovered things I had never seen before, like the long white envelope that in red pen read, "To Nimi, to Be Opened on the Occasion of My Death." Nimi is a nickname for my mother. But she wasn't there; they weren't even married anymore, so I opened it.

Dated March 28, 1997, almost two and a half years to the day before they announced their separation, he wrote, "Well, it finally happened. If you're reading this, it means that I'm dead. And I can't really say that I'm all that sorry. I had a good life—mostly in the years I spent with you. We had uncountable fights, but there was an underlying foundation of love and friendship and knowing that we could count on each other. And I love you for that and so much more. But when I wrote that I'm not all that sorry that I'm gone, I meant that I had a lot of pain in my life. Most of it was physical—bad feet that gave me pain every day of my life; a wrenching pain in my back that I felt every morning and, on some days, all day and night long; the subconscious threat of another aneurysm; the diabetes that I could not, or would not, control completely. Part of it was emotional—I really did hate living in Cleveland and would have much preferred a warmer climate, particularly in my later years." The rest of the letter never elaborated at all on the emotional pain and instead was a plea, urging my mother to use any money she was left with to help me pay back graduate student loans so I wouldn't be saddled with debt forever. And then he concluded the letter by saying, "If it is possible to love after death, please know that I love you now more than ever. And if there's life after death, I hope I don't see you too soon."

My father was a man who lived so many of his days talking about what he could have, should have, or would have done differently—about anything, even where to go for dinner or a plan he made—so it was startling and reassuring to read in this letter that he felt he had a good life and was accepting death, though of course that was written seven years before he became truly incapacitated. Until I found that letter, he had always struck me as the professional master in persuading others to avoid regret and the personal master in managing and manipulating regret. After all, in his work, he penned the famous line for Clairol, "If I've only one life to live, let me live it as a blonde." And with my mom and me, he constantly expressed regret and apologies for things he had done, begging for another chance to love and be loved.

In late June 2012, a few weeks before I moved from Boston to South Carolina and about six weeks before my dad died, I had to sign hospice papers for him. The staff predicted he would die within a month or two, and they were exactly right. My dad died on August 13, 2012. He had lost fifteen pounds in May and was referred to as having "failure to thrive," a description that up until that point, I thought was reserved only for infants. So dying seemed to be the obvious next step. He couldn't continue like he was. I had worried since I was little that he would die, but at the same time, I also somehow believed he would live forever.

My mother tells me that even when her dad was sick in the hospital for eighty days, she didn't quite realize or admit to herself that he was dying: "It's like I thought he would just go on and on and on." This is precisely what I thought about my dad as well. Even more strangely—and stupidly, perhaps—I *still* feel this way about my mother. I worry all the time that something will happen to her; I imagine how I will learn the news, where I will be, if I will get to be by her side or if I will learn it over the phone from her partner, Allan, or from a friend of hers, a stranger or a health care professional. I wonder and then worry about whether she will have to suffer so long like my dad did or if she will just drop dead. I wonder if things will turn out like they did with her mother who had Alzheimer's, that holy hell of diseases. For my grandmother's eightieth birthday, we got her an answering machine, since she was very social and active, and she absolutely loved it. Once she got sick and was moved into the nursing home, the aides helped her play back the messages, and she spoke back to the recorded voices, thinking they were on the phone with her at that moment. Another time, she pointed to a picture of my grandfather, the love of her life, whom she had by her side for more than fifty years, and was adamant it was the pope. And there were all the times where my mom called my grandmother at the nursing home and the aides claimed to bring her the phone, but she didn't even utter a sound; they also reported that my grandmother smiled when she heard it was my mom on the phone, yet my mother never believed they even told her she called.

This was my grandmother who, though she lived less than two miles from us as I was growing up, used to call my mother multiple times a day and, when they hung up, called back with still one more thing to say. She would call to meticulously describe every aspect of a dinner party she had just been to, every bit of the luscious food, every detail of the table settings and the linens. She called my mother to tell her the latest news about her friends, who was sick, who just died. She called to ask about recipes and to tell my mom about the volunteer committee she was part of at the hospital. About the Cleveland Orchestra performance she attended with her friend the night before. About her Hebrew lessons. About missing my grandfather. Right after my grandpa died, my mother invited my grandmother over for dinner every night so she wouldn't be alone. A woman who had eaten dinner and gone to bed with her husband for fifty-something years was suddenly alone. Death is so absolute, so black and white. That may be part of my problem in wrapping my head around it and actually comprehending it. I have never been a black-and-white thinker. Grief, as it evolves, is almost easier for me to understand despite how impossible and crazy it feels; grief is all gray matter.

In my mind, I fast-forward to the horrific day when I will still have so much to tell my mom and when she will be either gone in her mind or truly gone for good. And yet I don't believe it, can't believe it, don't want to believe it. That this woman who left teaching for a few years to have me, who wanted to be the one to stay home to give me baths, to feed me, to talk to me all day, might one day not even know who I am.

I figured my dad would go on and on because that had been the story all my life. Too often he moved from one health crisis to another. He either emerged victorious from one or learned how to manage the pain and hassle of it. So I had some reason to believe my dad would be okay, would go on, even from the biggest setbacks, like the Christmas night he spent in the emergency room, right after he fell on the ice at Cleveland Hopkins International Airport and broke his hip. I still thought to myself that maybe later in the week, he would be stable enough so we could all go on our planned trip to Delray Beach, Florida. I have no idea how I could have thought that. I imagine it was my brain anticipating how to protect my ever more scared heart. Then the next morning, I talked to the doctor on the phone, and he expressed concern that my dad wouldn't make it through hip surgery and that his heart would likely give out on the operating table. I was immediately catapulted back into the worry that he would die. In less than twenty-four hours, I went from "We're still going to all be able to go to Florida" to "He's going to die today." What I was less prepared for was living what would be many years with my dad in this murky space of being so unwell but still alive. I called my dear college friend Leslie the day he was having hip surgery, and she said, "Oh, Deb, a hip break is such a life-changing event." I really had no idea.

When my father got sick, he no longer chronicled his own days. With around-the-clock care at home, the health aides recorded the day's events, the major aches and pains, the distress, the medicine intake, and the bodily output—the color of the urine, the texture of the stools. I read records now about the days in February 2005 when he had urine the color of jewels, not yellow topaz as it is supposed to be, but more like rubies, garnets, and dark amber.

Once in the nursing home, he didn't even have a need to have his own datebooks. Instead, printed on large, legal-size paper and posted to corkboards were the calendars for all the residents. On these sheets, the staff seemed to want to count everything as an activity—even delivery of the newspaper, as though that was a major event.

When my friend Tom and I talked about the nursing home activities, we joked that it was like a preschool or overnight camp for geriatrics. There was the collage making, the manicures, the popcorn and movies, bingo, the banana split socials, the depressing picnics, the very bad musical performances, the occasional outing to a Chinese restaurant, the church services, the rosary prayers, taking communion, and the Bible studies. I hated when they sent copies of the calendar to me with the newsletter. Where had I left my father?

My dad was the only Jew in the final nursing home in which he ended up. None of the religious activities listed in the calendar even acknowledged that anything other than Christianity existed. There were residents who found this comforting, of course, like the woman who kept repeating at meals, "Thank you, Jesus. Thank you, Jesus," which drove my father crazy. And there was the birthday card that the nursing home ministry sent my father that drove *me* crazy that read, "Happy birthday to you! You are special to Jesus and special to us. God's love never fails." After that, I promptly called the home and told them that while I understood these were well intended, to please stop sending them.

It seemed like the only activity my dad enjoyed participating in at the nursing home was bingo. So when I visited, I tried to make it there for those two o'clock games on Mondays and Fridays. Bingo helped pass the time. They always gave out prizes, and my dad always wanted to win me something. It reminded me of all the times he had taken me to amusement parks when I was little and he wanted to win giant stuffed animals for me. Those carnival games are pure torture for the adults; there's more at stake for them.

It is obligatory for any good parent to at least try to win something for their kid, no matter what it is. At the time, those stuffed animals seemed plush and fabulous, though in reality, I knew I got better quality stuffed animals on vacation or from toy stores. But even back then I was excited that my dad wanted to win big for me, and I felt terrible for him if and when he lost.

At the nursing home, my dad had that same drive to win stuff for me as he did all those years ago. I couldn't bear to admit how cheesy and shoddy those prizes were, like even more grotesque and sadder versions of the stuffed animals at the amusement park; they weren't at all cuddly or cute. But somehow, I still wanted him to win them for me. I sensed what was at stake. I wanted him to again win big at something and feel hugely, whoppingly proud—a successful advertising executive on Medicaid. In a wheelchair. On too much prescription medicine. With skin flaking from his forehead. Swollen feet and blood bruises on his arms. Wearing adult diapers and stained clothes. With a bright plastic warning bracelet on his wrist stating, "Fall precautions required." Moving the bingo chips with unsteady hands and grimy, too-long fingernails. But still able to yell, "Bingo!" To win his only fortysomething daughter a pink bear or a charm or some flowery notepaper. Here, he finally had a shot at something again. To make his own fate when it seemed everyone had been making it for him.

9

The Gold Pen

I hate yellow gold. I always have. It looks gaudy and cheap to me. My skin is pale, my eyes green, and my hair almost black, and silver looks better on me. I like wearing chunky silver bracelets, cuffs, or bangles and a few big silver rings with African motifs. I also hate thin pens, the ones that are hard to grip. I prefer thicker pens, the ones that others seem to dislike because they write more like magic markers. So I am not sure why I've always been obsessed with my dad's pen. It's gold, it's thin, it's one of those fancy Cross pens that businessmen have used for decades—the powerful kind of pens that close deals, sign contracts, and make things happen. In my dad's case, he made a living wrestling with words, arranging them just right into catchy ad campaigns. With his pen, he scoured others' prose and made relentless revisions of others' ideas. More privately, he wrote my mom and me love letters and poetry, hate mail, and then apology letters.

On July 12, 2012, the movers came to box up my stuff in Boston to move me to South Carolina. The plan was that they would then load everything onto the moving truck, and on July 15, I would get on a plane with one suitcase, my backpack, and my mother, who agreed to join me to help me unpack and get settled in my new home. I had decided it would be wise to pack certain things myself—like the contents of my jewelry box where I had been keeping my dad's pen—but the packers convinced me that the more I allowed them to pack and transport for me, the better. I tend to over-pack anyway, so this made sense. I found an oversized red silk drawstring jewelry bag, dumped the contents of the jewelry box into it, and handed it to one of the men.

I arrived in Bluffton, South Carolina, and a few days later, so did my stuff—all 149 boxes, as well as my Nissan Sentra. As I unpacked, some things surprised me, things I had not used in Boston with my ex-husband Mark, things from my dad's place that I had stored in boxes in our basement—slides from childhood trips to Europe, my childhood diaries, letters that my grandmother had written to me, letters that my mother had written to my father, and so many photographs. I was intrigued by figuring out how to repurpose my furniture and objects in a new home, in different rooms from where they had been used before. That spirit of reinvention always inspires me.

My mother and I started to unpack my bedroom, but I couldn't find the pen in the jewelry bag. I started to unpack my study and set up small colorful pails of pens and pencils on my desk, the same desk my father used years ago, and I still could not find the pen. How could I suddenly have lost the one thing that I had held onto for more than seven years since my dad had been sick? How could I have been that careless and disorganized? How was it possible that I had doubles and triples of some things and every pashmina, every book, and way too many spatulas, and yet I could not find this pen? How had I managed to lose the one thing that seemed most emblematic of my dad, that tethered me to his work and the life of his mind?

I understood that my dad lost his mind—after all, that's what the diagnosis of dementia is all about—but I had not lost my memory of my dad's mind, with all its crevices of brilliance, darkness, and madness. All I wanted was his pen. For me, it represented the link to a writing life, a creative life, a juicy life, and a prosperous life. It was also a link to my dad's healthier days, an evocative object that helped me recall his vigor, vitality, and robustness. Of course, I had other objects I knew he used or enjoyed when he was living independently, but many were objects of leisure. My dad's words are what I remembered most and still do, and I believed this pen to be the tool he used to craft and mix and blend words. That is what I longed for.

Pens also remind me of a time when we were all less tethered, a time when a machine wasn't the mediating force between the brain and the hand and the words on the page. I intuited that I might never use this pen to actually write. I just wanted it around to anchor me to creativity—to my dad's and to mine.

I remember how my dad looked hunkered down over the oversized dining table in our house, working late into the night on advertising slogans and marketing presentations for prospective clients due the very next day, with multiple yellow legal pads spread all over and his gold pen. I can still see the way his right hand gripped the pen and his left hand gently, yet with a sense of firmness, held the paper in place. With his head cocked slightly to the left, all that was obvious to me was how the words looked as if they effortlessly flowed out of my father and onto the paper. Occasionally, he made notes on the margins of the papers for his secretary so she would know to flip the paper over and follow the arrows for inserting section A, B, or C. This was the 1970s and '80s, before my dad used a computer, with its cut and paste functions. But even back then, if you read my dad's work over in its entirety, it was seamless. In my mind, the whole scene conjures up an intense sense of work and procrastination.

I relate to this. In college, I often worked on papers until two, three, or four o'clock in the morning that were due that same day and have retained something of my topsy-turvy twentysomething routine even today. Now I'm much less apt to procrastinate, but I still live an erratic schedule. In recent years, I have tried writing in the mornings and afternoons, yet there is still something about the night, the way creativity seems to linger about more quietly yet swirls around more urgently and magically, that pulls me in, that gives me a surge. My father was critical of my schedule, thinking I stayed up far too late and slept too much of the day away, and I often internalize that same criticism even today, wishing in some ways that I was a true morning person. Perhaps he was trying to get me to learn from what he perceived to be his own shortcomings.

But the iconic image I hold of my dad, propped up at that table, committed to resisting sleep, with his pen in the middle of the night, simultaneously moves me and arrests me—my dad at one with the pen. The relationship between them is reassuring in its durability and reliability yet unsettling in its relentless quest for perfection.

Two summers before I moved to my new home in South Carolina, Craig, my dad's psychologist, called and asked me to bring slides to the nursing home for my dad to see, so I loaded up the trunk of the car with boxes of slide carousels, rented a projector, and made the drive to Cleveland. I didn't know it then, but that marked the last visit I would ever have with my father. A talented photographer with a keen eye, my dad had taken all of these pictures through the years, and Craig thought this would be a good activity for us to share together. Craig, my dad, and I made our way to the family lounge to go through the slides. Some were from childhood trips with my parents to the French Riviera, the English countryside, Scandinavia, Italy, Carmel, Big Sur, and Maine.

Others were pictures from concerts, botanical gardens, and museums. I was concerned about what it would mean for my dad to be inundated with all these images and how it would impact him. As it turns out, the projector did not work, and we were unable to view the slides. Craig wheeled my dad upstairs while I loaded everything back into the car. When I returned to my father's room to find them, Craig took me aside and quietly whispered, "Your dad broke down a little." I asked, "Why? What did he say?" Craig told me that my dad said, "You're not gonna leave me, are you?" and then suddenly Craig burst into tears, covered his mouth with his hand, and ran out of the room and down the hall. I felt compassion for his sense of embarrassment crying as a therapist, for his need to rush away from me. I wondered if there might be unconscious father/son dynamics going on and potential countertransference issues for him in letting go of my dad. I definitely related to his reaction, because there are times in my own work, particularly when I teach college students about violent trauma and its effects, that I see how the material resonates with so many of my students' life experiences, and I hold back tears, cry, or speak with a broken voice, with a broken heart.

Looking back, I was always caught up in my dad's writing, and especially in its slickness and precision, qualities that went missing upon my dad's diagnosis of dementia. I remember visiting him at the dinner hour on a Sunday night at a different nursing home in Cleveland, probably in 2006 or so. He was seated with a woman named Rose. The other woman assigned to the table was Ann, but she was not there that night. Her son, Fred, and daughter-in-law, Joan, had come to take her home for dinner. This is something I was unable to do since I visited from Boston. After dinner, we were all hanging around in the lounge area, and Joan approached us. She had just dropped Ann back at her room, and she went into detail about what she had prepared for dinner: they had steaks on the grill, sugar snap peas, and sweet potatoes, and for dessert, they had mango sorbet, cantaloupe, and berries. It sounded healthy, colorful, and bountiful. On behalf of my dad, I was thoroughly envious. I longed for him to have this sort of meal, either home-cooked or in a great restaurant. I wish I could have regularly afforded to take him out for dinner, but to do so, I would have needed to hire an aide to help. All of this was cost prohibitive in the midst of my search for a tenure-track job in higher education, juggling both mounting student loans and crushing credit card debt. I was faced with a far more limited financial landscape than the one in which I grew up. The whole thing was like a bad sequel to the '90s indie film *Slums of Beverly Hills*, with this one called something like *Going on Medicaid in Beachwood, Ohio*, a tragicomedy in which I have come to understand social class as fluid and dynamic, nervously shifting in the course of one's lifetime.

Joan asked my dad what he had for dinner. He did not respond. I thought to myself, "But, Dad, you just had dinner an hour and a half ago. You used to be able to recall meals you had months and years ago in fancy restaurants." Fred says, "Jim, you don't remember?" So as to compensate for any potential embarrassment, I jumped right in: "Oh, yeah, my dad had matzo ball soup, a small salad, pot roast, mixed vegetables, boiled potatoes, and marble cake."

As we were all talking, the nursing aide brought my dad neon orange peanut butter crackers as a snack. My dad's hands shook as he tried to release the plastic surrounding the crackers just as they shook when he ate his dinner. The image I remember from that dinner is still haunting—my dad had trouble stabbing the grape tomatoes on his salad. I still recall how he used his left hand to hold the tomato still and then tried to steady the fork in his right hand to prick the tomato.

Yet twenty-five years before that, during an argument at a dinner party with my mother's parents, he threw plates in the kitchen with great precision. On better, calmer days, he grasped his pen with ease, still dreaming up sharp, pointed ad campaigns. But the tomato—that small ball of fleshy, juicy, red matter—was out of his reach, out of his control. And then even the conversation began to lack precision and self-control as he remarked to me, "I wish I could shower with you again. When you were a baby, you would get naked, and I would wear a bathing suit, and I would take you in the shower." And then completely out of context, he turned to Fred and said, "Bananas give me gas."

From about 2000 until 2006, my dad used his pen less and less and started to transition to using an iMac, that now retro-looking machine with the blueberry-colored sides, not exactly the choice of most men in their late seventies, but he possessed an aesthetic all his own. After 2006, steeped in the confusion of dementia, he stopped using both the computer and the pen.

I spent the months following my move to South Carolina believing that only if and when I ever found the pen again would I be able to write. As a result, my creativity felt conditional at best. At some point, I stumbled upon an old favorite book by Carolyn Heilbrun, *Writing a Woman's Life*, in which she is critical of this line of thinking as being ultimately self-punishing: "We women have lived too much with closure: 'if he notices me, if I marry him, if I get into college, if I get this work accepted, if I get this job'—there always seems to loom the possibility of something being over, settled, sweeping clear the way for contentment. This is the delusion of a passive life. When the hope for closure is abandoned, when there is an end to fantasy, adventure for women will begin."[1] I decided to try to tame my self-expectations about finding the pen. After all, clearly it was gone. Inspired by Buddhist teachings that it is best not to cling, to not be too attached, I tried to live out the mantra "Not too tight, not too loose."

In the late fall of 2012, I became interested in dating again and very reluctantly joined Match.com. It seemed to be the only way to meet anyone. I was sick of being hit on by seventy-something wealthy retired golfers at the Starbucks near Hilton Head. This online dating world is where my dad's craft would really shine. He would have had me neatly and crisply packaged with a great photo and tagline and a nifty description of what I was seeking in a relationship. If nothing else, we'd have gotten a good laugh out of the whole thing, and he would have been amused by the terrible self-marketing of others. So I took a chance, and I met Mike. We spent an entire month emailing and calling until our first date on December 1, 2012. We arranged to meet for lunch at noon and wound up leaving each other after 11 p.m. Later that same week, I shared relationship advice with a former student who became a friend and told her, "The real litmus test is if you never want the conversation to end."

An English major, a director of media relations, a former radio reporter, a music buff, a lover of wordplay, and an avid reader, Mike is no stranger to the significance of words and the power of voice. He isn't like my father at all, but there are some basic similarities between the two men: both possess a bold, strong, energetic voice and appreciate a good story; a great tagline; and a catchy, memorable slogan. A few days after our first date, Mike and I were talking on the phone about aging, dementia, and abuse, and I shared with him a bit about my dad. I briefly mentioned the fact that this had become the subject of much of my writing. The next day he emailed me indicating an interest in reading my work if I was up for sharing it. So later that day, I sent him my first gritty essay about caregiving for my dad that had just been accepted for publication. I figured the quality of writing seemed decent enough, that the content would either make him interested to know more about me or be completely off-putting and make him run like hell. Either way, these seemed like good things for me to learn early on—to know if he could sit through that level of discomfort, really be there, talk about it, ask questions, and still want to stay. In some ways perhaps I was testing him. His gracious response to that first essay, the one that would eventually become the chapter "Sugar" in this book, and his curiosity to know more about me ignited in me a desire to write more, to get my work out; it made me gutsier about my writing, the way I longed to be.

Every morning since December 1, 2012, with the exception of the mornings we are able to wake up together on weekends and vacations, Mike has sent me an email. However, I have never received words on paper, neither a card nor a letter. The tiny cards that accompany the flowers he has sent don't count because it's not his writing. Other than seeing him sign his name on a restaurant bill or tally up my losing score when we play UNO, I have very little idea what his handwriting really looks like. There seems to be nothing about how we function that relies on a pen. On words, yes, many of them. But not on pens. Perhaps it is indeed possible to write, and live, and love without the pen.

I have long been intrigued with silence and solitude, but I do not always set aside the time for it that I know is nourishing. In August 2012, I finally decided to make time to read Anne LeClaire's *Listening below the Noise: The Transformative Power of Silence.* A woman minister sitting next to me on an airplane had recommended it. LeClaire talks about her journey in practicing full days of silence, essentially letting go of the surface chatter of the world to venture into the depths of her own being. This resonates with me. I know that in stillness there is greater light and clarity for living a more expansive, profound, creative, and spacious life. What hadn't yet registered with me was how that same stillness and quiet is necessary for dying. LeClaire recalls a story of a friend's husband who said when nearing the end of his life, "I'm dying. Dying requires concentration. It requires quiet."[2]

Standing at the ticket counter at the Savannah airport on August 13, 2012, ready to check in for a flight to Cleveland to have my last goodbye with my dad, I received a call from hospice that he had just died. I fell to the floor sobbing. It was as though my dad had left me midsentence. How do we finish the narrative of our lives without our parents? Minutes later, I overheard a young boy, about eight years old, ask his mom, "Do you know where Dad is?" I wanted to scoop the kid up and say, "You know, honey, I have the exact same question."

On the last day of my father's life, he stopped speaking, and I have come to believe that with his urgent desire to protect me, he would not let me see him that way, nor would he let me interact with him in the absence of words. My dad and I were never really quiet around each other. It was only when he lived in nursing homes that we experienced more quiet together than ever before. While he slept or while the nurses assisted him, I got into a habit of always having with me a tote bag filled with papers to grade, books to read, and a legal pad to jot down notes about this whole experience of caregiving for an ill and elderly parent who had been abusive. So much confused me, and writing seemed like a way to sort through the muck, to let the grime of the experience fall out of me and away from me. Writing was a way out and a way in.

Alternating between my dad's naps, hallucinations, and jarring moments of lucidity, I sat and stared at him, wept, studied his face and his body and the room, and compulsively wrote with one of my own thick pens on a legal pad. Never on my laptop as I did not bring it on my trips. Somehow, the words that best captured how I felt only revealed themselves in front of him. It was as though as he continually lost his grasp of language, I was able to more fully come into my own sense of voice about our experience.

In the spring of 2009, I wrote this as my dad took a nap:

I watch you as you sleep, not unlike you probably watched me as I slept as a newborn baby and as a young girl. In wonder, in awe, in calm, and in worry. A parent watches a child sleep with anticipation of a future. An adult child watches a sick parent sleep with a sense of the past. You are finally still and quiet, you, a man who I know as chaotic and loud. We rest in this calm as you fall in and out of slumber and I grade papers. I need to study your face, memorize it, as I know I'll need it one day, yet the you now is not the you I want to remember. In a few days, I'll be back with over a hundred students, giving lectures, attending meetings, going to a concert, a lunch with a friend, a performance of *The Vagina Monologues*, and in my week ahead, I worry about being too busy, about running from one activity to the next, breathless, yet one day, Daddy, you did this too, right? How would you restructure those days now? What did you hope for? What do you hope for now? With your tongue half out of your mouth, you resemble a little boy with Down syndrome. You look tired, though I can't tell if you're tired of this life. Yesterday I brought you coffee from Caribou with one of their napkins that made a jab at Starbucks that said, "Our coffee is smooth and fresh 'cause burnt and bitter were already taken." Whenever I see great lines and logos, I think of you. Your creativity still shines through as we leaf through *Metropolitan Home* and marvel at minimalist spaces. Your stained maroon sweatpants are pulled up halfway toward your chest, and your stomach looks distended. Earlier today, I saw as you put imaginary pills to your mouth with your fingers, something I assumed to be a self-soothing ritual you performed after the nurse told you it was not yet time for more medication. Being in Cleveland, I'm surrounded by childhood friends hanging out with their dads, younger men than you, in their sixties and early seventies, robust, athletic, energetic men vigorously playing tennis and golf, working, traveling, and chasing after their dreams, not figments of their imaginations in thin air. Oh, Daddy. Your eyes open suddenly and you ask, "What are you writing?" I quickly respond, "Oh, nothing really, it's just for school."

However, writing about my dad in front of my dad seemed like a profound act of betrayal. It also felt mean. As I see it now, it helped me grieve and let go. Contained in a tight, unattractive physical space with my dad, enmeshed in his care in ways I probably should have never been, I was writing to untangle a knotty family narrative, to finally record and understand my experience as my own. By writing in front of him, I think something else happened that was necessary. I came to realize that all we had to give to each other was space. Psychic space. Most importantly, I needed to give him space and quiet to eventually die. My dad's almost eight years of debilitating illness made me grasp his final inability to help and guide me, and that gave me the space I needed to dream of what I wanted to do. Though he helped me and was involved in most major decisions I had made in my life, dementia forced him to check out. It also forced me to check in with how well I was writing my own life.

One day, a little more than two years before he died, he asked me, "Deb, what does 'quiet' mean and how do you spell it?" Of all the words to pick, to ask about, I was floored. Quiet is a word that small children know. How could my dad be eighty-two years old and unable to process this simple word?

But it felt tremendously revealing; this was my dad, with his loud voice and mean bark, though people also remarked that he had a great voice. Even in his eighties, he often sounded much more youthful. His voice was all at once soothing, booming, gentle, and loving—and it was always clear.

I value what's involved in cultivating one's voice. Feminist politics and my antiviolence work have always led me back to the power of finding one's voice. I think voice is both the quality of how we speak as well as what we speak about from a gut level of clarity and wholeness. On my fortieth birthday, my dad left me a gorgeous voice mail in which he told me he loved being my father; I obsessively recorded it in various places so I would be sure to always have it. While I am fortunate to have an uncanny memory for voices anyway, his voice is one I want to hear again, and not just in my head.

I have heard that it's in the silence that we most come to know another person and ourselves. Six weeks before my dad died, the nursing home called me, wanting my signature to get my dad into hospice. All the years of worrying about how and when they would call to tell me he died were replaced in my head with "He's dying; it's happening now." I asked to speak with him. I really just found myself wanting his advice more than anyone else's, and I said, "I want you to know I love you, Dad." I tried to say it in a way that he wouldn't be fully aware that I knew he was dying. He replied, "You don't need to worry about that, Deb; I know you do." I then asked him, "What's your advice for me, Dad, for anything in the world?" I so desperately wanted his input, maybe even his criticisms to weigh against my own perceptions and judgment. Sometimes in the past, he would say, "It's your life, Deb; live it." And then, for the first time, he said nothing. There was dead air. Not a word. Just blank space. I thought, "Wait, Dad, for decades you wanted to tell me what to do and how to do it and now I actually want and need your advice and you aren't going to give it?" Then suddenly, this became oddly reassuring and liberating for me. Finally, there was no dictating, no steering, no telling me what to do more of, what to do less of, criticizing what decisions I made, threatening me, or shouting or swearing at me at the top of his lungs. His parting gift to me was the absence of all that. There was just quiet space, an odd silence of acceptance and connection. And in that space, there was freedom for me. Perhaps the air wasn't dead but more alive and full of possibility for me to recraft my life than ever before. To write my life into being, into meaning. The legacy he left me with was that.

On a Wednesday in late February 2013, I was packing up at the end of my Introduction to Sociology class. Caitlin, one of my students, approached me to explain why she had so many absences. Before she started talking, I went to put away the washable markers that I had been using on the whiteboard in class. I stuck them in a small pouch that I never seemed to use and suddenly found myself touching something thin and familiar. I looked down and saw the gold pen. I didn't even recall putting it there, but it makes sense that I must have, since the backpack was my carry-on luggage for the plane, for all the things I most definitely did not want to risk losing in the move. I smiled at myself deep within my very being, in that way that was not visible on my face but where my heart felt profound gratitude and relief. My dad had always wanted to see me teach a class and never got the chance; he wanted to move to the Carolinas and never did. And suddenly, right there was my dad. In my classroom in South Carolina. I wanted to either laugh hysterically or cry, but I knew what I had to do in that moment: I had to talk to Caitlin. I had already learned to begin to write a life without the pen: a life full of new love and intense possibility.

Caitlin told me, "I am so sorry I haven't made it to class, See, it's just that my friend shot and killed himself, and this is all on top of my dad dying a few months ago, just like you, Deb." Grief often tugs really hard. I was suddenly struck by what students remember of what we tell them, what they relate to, how so much of what's important for them is not the pure academic stuff but the life stuff, the survival skills. During the course of the year, I had become more open about how my dad had died just days before school started, how I was divorced, how I had grown up in an emotionally abusive home. I was feeling an extraordinary pull to not sugarcoat reality.

Caitlin began to cry and then told me that she was worried about caring for her little sister, since her mother had a heart attack within days of her father's death due to the stress of it all. It hit me that Caitlin was just eighteen, that I was forty-three, perhaps about the age of her mother. I thought I was too young to lose my father, that this man so deeply lodged in the world, in my world, was gone far too soon. I was certain Caitlin was too young to lose her father. Instinctively, I reached out to hug Caitlin, and we exchanged very few words; quiet presence through this pain was all that was necessary. I lightly touched her on her face as she cried. I completely let go of what is supposedly appropriate in a professional, academic context. This immediately reminded me of Craig, the therapist at the nursing home.

All that I clung to was what seemed right in that moment of deepened vulnerability for Caitlin and for me. I have learned that if I throw the whole of myself into teaching, the students learn more, and so do I. I have also learned that teaching and learning can heal. Healing only happens from the rawness that's exposed. I reminded Caitlin that I was there if she needed any resources—anything, really. But we were headed into spring break, and she vanished soon after that. She'll never know how serendipitous it was for me to share newly found father loss and to find that pen all in the space of one tiny conversation.

I left campus, jumped into my car, and immediately called Mike. "You'll never believe this. I just found the pen," I exclaimed, and then I chuckled and said, "And I even think there's a story in here, something about how I'm glad that I found it but even more glad that I first had to figure out how to let it go."

Notes

1. Carolyn G. Heilbrun, *Writing a Woman's Life* (New York: Ballantine, 1988), 130.
2. Anne D. LeClaire, *Listening below the Noise: The Transformative Power of Silence* (New York: Harper Perennial, 2009), 149.

10

The Volunteer

In late 2003, my father enrolled in a quantum mechanics class. I am not convinced it was because he was truly a life-long learner per se. He was looking for a way to stay sharp and to be the best in the class. Then in early 2004, he decided to volunteer at a school to help kids read and do math. I always found that a strange choice, because when he helped me with homework when I was growing up, he was impatient with me, unwilling to see me do anything less than perfectly. Around the same time as he was volunteering, he got involved with John Kerry's campaign for president. He was also philanthropic, donating a good deal of money to an organization for women with cancer and attending their events. He was dating at the time, and I think giving to this organization was his way to impress women, to show them he was doing good things in the community. It seemed to work especially well with the women he dated who had survived breast cancer. All of this activity happened shortly before my dad fell and broke his hip and his whole life went tumbling down along with it, making it so I never learned how any of these activities and projects really ended or what he decided to follow through on or not.

I think he was desperately looking for a way to give shape, purpose, and meaning to those emptier days after retirement and trying to adjust to a life without my mother. And I think he was searching for redemption. That became most apparent to me even earlier, at the end of August 2000, not even a year after he and my mom split. My dad called me in Boston and left me a voice mail proudly declaring that he had just returned from an introductory session for potential volunteers at a program in Cleveland aimed at ending domestic violence and child abuse. At that time in my life, I was busy pursuing a doctorate degree and working a part-time yet fully consuming job as a counselor and clinical supervisor in a battering intervention program. My dad left two messages at 11 p.m., one at 12:45 a.m., and another at 1:15 a.m. The first message was tender and loving, and he sounded excited to share about this new adventure with me. He wanted me to be proud, or at the very least interested. Within just a couple of hours, by message number three, he was berating me for not being home. The ironic fact of his demanding, narcissistic behavior immediately following his session at the agency was not lost on me. Here I was, thirty years old, with surveillance and a curfew imposed from more than six hundred miles away and his continued insistence that he be the center of my universe.

The evening my dad called to tell me all this, I was out at my friend Susan's house for a fabulous, authentic Mexican meal. Having lived a long time in New Mexico, she knew how to make killer enchiladas. Susan and I met through our work at the intervention program. She's a formerly battered woman whose ex-husband had never successfully finished the program. She was a tireless advocate for women who had been hurt, and she was relied on as an expert to train employees and volunteers in how to do partner contacts so we could reach out to abused partners and ex-partners of the men we were counseling to give them updates on the men's progress in the groups and to provide answers to questions they might have to help heighten their safety.

I had stayed to talk with Susan into the wee hours of the morning—she told the best stories. Susan is a few decades older than I am; she could be my mother. And she's an "othermother," a friend with life experience and wisdom, more like a mentor. She listened intently when I talked and helped me brainstorm about my dissertation as well as about my horrible adviser, the one who was an expert at making me feel like I wasn't good enough, the one I had to deal with before I had the guts to switch advisers. I got feedback from Susan about my writing, and we dreamed about how to get funding for artistic projects to aid in healing women affected by violence. But my dad saw my being out so late as proof that I was doing nothing toward finishing my PhD, and he threatened to cut me off from some of the money he was giving me to get me through the program. I listened to his escalating impatience and anger on my machine and could not believe that he was verbally abusing me the very same day he had been at this center for domestic violence.

In the morning, I calmly returned my dad's phone calls. He said that he was the only man who showed up to the training. I know full well that when men appear in these sorts of centers and settings, they occasionally garner suspicion, but more likely they receive unearned praise—they are revered as "the good one," "the good man." This valorization of men who just show up is hard for women to endure who have worked in the movement to end violence against women for so many years. When men do work that is regarded as feminist, they are listened to, paid more, and celebrated, even if their life actions aren't feminist; when women do feminist work, they are most often vilified.

Then my dad exclaimed, "The funniest thing happened, honey. Shannon, the woman leading the training, looks just like you . . . you know, your same kind of curly, wavy hair and those big, gorgeous eyes of yours. I mean, it was wild; she could have been your twin sister." As we have established, I am an only child. However, I am often told I look "just like someone else" or specifically like either the comedienne Rita Rudner, though I wish I was as hilarious, or the young version of Liz Taylor, though I wish I was as rich—oh, and also able to reinvent myself with so many men so many times. Apparently, my dad was so intrigued with this resemblance that he showed Shannon a photo of me from his wallet, and she said to him, likewise stunned by the resemblance, "What are you doing with a picture of me?"

He went on to tell me that he was not sure how realistic it would be to ultimately volunteer because of the time commitment involved to train to be on the hotline. *The hotline. That thing for crisis calls, for women in distress.* These trainings average around forty hours. My mind was catapulted to a possible time in the future when a woman in crisis would call and *my father* would answer the phone. In what universe would this even be possible? This just seemed patently ridiculous. Sure, he had a great, smooth voice. Years ago, he even hosted a radio show called *Jim and Jazz.* He might momentarily soothe and comfort a crying woman. But suddenly, I wondered if he thought he might meet women this way—vulnerable women he could impress, prey on, date, buy fancy things for, take to extravagant places for dinner, and leave even more needy for sustenance.

He found one forty-hour training difficult to commit to. I've done umpteen trainings, volunteered in this world of crisis and fear and despair for thousands of hours since I was twenty-one and spent countless hours agonizing and analyzing about abuse with clients and in my own therapy.

My dad's own behavior and its consequences largely created my need to do all this work. I literally lost time in my own life, and my dad was worried he couldn't find the time in his. I didn't want him to work in an agency like one specializing in antiviolence work, and I really wanted it to be because someone in charge there saw my dad's snow job for what it was and prohibited his attendance there, not because he claimed to not have the time. And why wasn't the center calling my mother and/or me to get our perspectives on my father? In my work in domestic violence, we always called the partners and ex-partners of people applying for jobs with us to have some check and balance on what they were like in a relationship. I never particularly liked doing these background checks; it felt intrusive. But as my dad considered doing this counseling work, the act of an agency not doing these intimate, exploratory interviews seemed shoddy and wrong. I knew these advocacy places routinely run CORI (criminal offender record information) checks on potential employees, but so much damage can be done before the law intervenes, if it ever does. And so much goes unreported. The CORI will tell staff if a person tried to rob a bank, but not someone's spirit; the CORI says if someone wrote bad checks, but not that they called someone they claim to love really bad names; the CORI says if the police were called because of a strangulation, but not whether someone casually threatened to kill their partner or children; a CORI will say if someone has a DUI, but not whether he drove recklessly with his wife and kid when he was irate, screaming with raised fists and nearly driving into a telephone pole. A lack of time seemed like such an excuse for my dad that I wasn't buying it. I wondered if maybe he realized on some gut level that he was not cut out for dealing with this depth of trauma and what it does to a person.

Abuse has a particular relationship with time. Abuse stunts a victim's growth and simultaneously speeds it up. However, the timelines for healing and recovery are different for the person hurt than the person who created the pain. Abusers I worked with would impatiently grumble, "But it happened a few months ago. Why isn't she over it by now?" Abusers seem to want to rush time. No wonder so many male abusers try to woo women into superfast courtships—it makes it harder and harder for the women to see any flaws. These men seduce at lightning speed. By rushing things, abusers rapidly blur the vision of their partners before the women can make fully informed choices about what is working in the relationship and what is not.

As a child, when I heard the story of my parents' first date, I thought it was romantic, like something out of a princess fantasy. Their mutual friends had set them up on a blind date. After dinner, in a swimming pool in Columbus, Ohio, on July 15, 1967, my father told my mother that he would marry her by the end of the year. He didn't really ask. He just told her this would happen. According to the story, she just laughed it off and told him he was crazy. Now it gives me the creeps to think that they got married on December 24, 1967, especially since I know that fast courtships are correlated with domestic violence—and worse, domestic homicide.

In thinking about time and abuse, I'm reminded of when Susan guest lectured in my family violence classes about her experience surviving violence. She posed powerful questions to my students: What would you do with all the time and energy you'd have if you weren't focused on working to end violence or working to get safe? How would this free you to be more creative in the world? How would those creative projects change the world?

I still think about my dad's excitement when he told me that I so closely resembled Shannon, the trainer at the domestic violence program where he almost volunteered. It's actually unbelievably fitting that we could look so strikingly similar. I doubt that my father looked into her big eyes and saw me in the same way I look into batterers' eyes and see him. Obviously, he made a physical connection with her, but did it stop there? Why? How could it not have run deeper for him? Was it merely time that he'd be losing by making the volunteer commitment? Or on some deep unconscious level, was the problem that he'd be losing the image in his mind of a very little girl, with piles of curly dark hair framing a face marked by huge, smoke-gray eyes, as he called them, looking up at him with adoration and glee or reflecting back at him in the car's rearview mirror, saying, "My daddy will do anything for me." There are my now horrified, worn eyes staring back at him in the body of a woman, seething and stirring, raging and loving, welcoming, open, embracing, shutting down and withholding, carefully negotiating the corners of girlhood and womanhood that never got entirely smoothed out. Witnessing horror, participating in it, keeps those corners rough, jagged, and ragged. By not being able to commit to what is involved in volunteering, was my father running from me, this girl-woman who might cross him, might hold him accountable? Was Shannon, this trainer, the look-alike woman, too reminiscent of all that he was running from?

For the years that I worked with violent men, it made my dad nervous. He expressed concern about my safety, about finishing groups at 10 p.m. and being at the program till 11 p.m. and getting to my car and driving home. He bought into the cultural narrative, the mythology, that it's the stranger in the bushes late at night that we should fear the most. He also bought into the idea that the men I worked with were slime buckets and scary monsters. Occasionally, I tried to explain to him—to no avail, of course—that most of these men were no different than he was, that they said and did some nasty, hurtful, and threatening things to the women and children in their lives but also had redeeming qualities, and that's why so many of those women and children wanted to stay in relationships with them. They wanted the violence to stop and the relationship to continue.

For a long time, I encouraged my dad to seek professional help. I thought it would do him some good in easing the transition after his divorce from my mom. I thought it might take the edge off what looked like depression, and I wanted him to get help for his abuse. But when he told me that he thought of volunteering in the domestic violence program without first getting the help he so desperately needed, I came head to head with my dad's limitations and realized he was never going to seek help for his abuse. He minimized and denied how his behavior played such an enormous role in the demise of his marriage to my mother and how it quite probably negatively impacted other intimate relationships he had with women I never knew. Somehow he thought he could do something productive by trying to help others in abusive relationships. It seemed as absurd as people with eating disorders wanting to work at weight loss centers before fully helping and healing themselves.

In October 2009 I went to visit my dad in the nursing home, a trip made to belatedly celebrate his birthday. We were sitting around talking, and out of the blue, he said, "Do you know much I liked to kiss your feet? I'd have you on the changing table when you were tiny and I'd lift up your little legs and chomp on your feet."

"Did I laugh?" I asked, and he replied, "Oh, yeah!"

Then his face stiffened and looked more serious, and he told me how sad he was that my grandma Bertie, his mother, wasn't nice to me. I tried to comfort him, to tell him I wasn't angry, that it was okay, that while I indeed experienced her as mean, crotchety, and nasty, I felt it was her loss. I also told him I wished I had met my grandpa Jack. He died right before I was born. I asked my father what their marriage was like. It was not until this moment that he acknowledged to me that his parents' marriage was so bad, they should have gotten divorced.

He shared a story with me about a time when he was a very little boy growing up in New Jersey and his mom took him to Atlantic City for the weekend alone. Jack often took in dogs and had just brought home two new dogs; Bertie only wanted one. When Bertie told Jack this, he slugged her and gave her two black eyes. Immediately, I wanted to ask my dad two questions, the same ones I asked the abusers I met when I ran counseling groups—with whom did he side, and did he step in to intervene? Apparently, he was too little to get involved, but he did say he sided with his mother.

Like my clients, he didn't want to see his mother or daughter hurt by a man, yet he ended up doing the same thing when he became a man. And as is true for so many abusers, apparently my grandfather had two different faces—a public one and a private one. He owned supermarkets, worked hard, and was successful, and people liked and respected him. Yet he was a tyrant at home. But my dad also explained that many people were aware of his father's mean streak and were upset by it. It was like my dad was describing himself. Perhaps there's a third face in abuse, aside from the strictly public and private ones—the one that is blended and messy, the private one that still rears its head publicly at times. "He'd just as soon slug you as talk to you," my dad said about his father. It's a sad vision thinking of my dad as a small boy, traveling with his mother badly injured at the hands of his father. I kept wondering what my great-grandfather did to Grandpa Jack when he was growing up, but I didn't ask. If we could have had this conversation years earlier, I would have probed further. But when a parent is in a nursing home and memories are tender, it feels mean to push the hurt.

My dad had always rationalized and justified his behavior by claiming he had a bad temper by insinuating that if my mother or I had done something or not done something, he would not have behaved the way he did. Like with most abusers, when he felt hurt, he made sure we felt hurt also. Seeing my dad in a wheelchair reflecting on his own mangled childhood made me see the ravages of abuse—and him—in a new way.

My dad's cousin was turning ninety-one during that same visit, and we called to wish her a happy birthday. When we got off the phone, I turned and asked my dad, "So you wanna live to be one hundred?"

"Nah," he said. "My goal is to get healthy and die." I laughed but didn't understand what he meant. "I just don't want to die like my parents did," he said.

Trapped in a body that could no longer move was a confused boy still wrestling with a sense of masculinity that was not serving him well. Because our conversation was embedded in concentric circles of end-of-life regrets and wishes, it was hard to untangle what he actually felt the most remorseful about.

When I teach about intimacy and violence or give public talks, I am often asked, "Do you think the abuser is sorry? Does he regret it? Can he change?" Most often, it's women who ask me this; I think they are hoping I will say yes in order to help them redeem the men who might have done them wrong. When I have done public readings, I am often asked, "Do you think your dad was sorry?" "Yes and no" is what I say. The murky grayness of ambiguity is the only thing that feels clear to me.

The activist in me wants to say no; if he was truly sorry, he would not have continued to be abusive. Or maybe he was just sorry for himself and what he lost, not sorry for the effects that his behavior had on others. He was smart and should have known better. He had a choice, and he made the wrong one. Those are the stock answers in the field. I could recite them at 3:00 a.m. in my sleep. But when I think about my father, these explanations all come up short. They don't really capture all the nuances of my father's behavior or my own feelings about it.

Abusers aren't some monolithic enemy. Any woman who has loved an abuser knows that best. There's much to love before we learn exactly what to hate. That's what makes emotionally abusive relationships so seductive and makes us so ready to run back to someone who has abused us before and try to work it out.

I believe there's a dialectic of rage—the abuser's perception of a loss of a control and a simultaneous desire to then wield power and control and the rage and resistance of the victim, however overt or subtle. These rages collide, implode, combust, and make new rage. We need to be ready to know and learn these men's stories. We need to grapple with the humanity of abusers as we do with the heinous quality of their crimes, and we should try to reconcile their desires and wishes as we weigh them against the often equally unmet desires and wishes of their victims. In talking to my dad that afternoon in the nursing home, my rage still lingered in the room, but it was less hot; it moved more slowly and with less urgency. It swirled with curiosity for the family members I never knew but who had helped form the father I was now caring for. And learning of a parent's unmet desires and wishes at the end of their life is almost too impossible to bear. It can't help but soften you. Do I still feel the rage now? It lurks about in the shadows and hides around corners. I can't touch it the way I used to. That's okay. I don't want to. But neither will I ever forget.

I also remember all the good parts. I am aware that death can often make the good parts look even better than they were and erase the bad parts. I choose to hold both, let them live side by side. I do this because both are true. And I think my waves of grief crash over the heavy rocks of my rage, eroding them bit by bit.

The Buddhist monk Thich Nhat Hanh tells the tragic story of a sea pirate who raped a young girl; consequently, she jumped in the ocean to drown herself. He explained that one couldn't simply, exclusively take the side of the girl. He says it's tempting but far too easy to just want to shoot the pirate. He insists that if we were born in the village of the pirate and raised under similar conditions, we, too, would likely become sea pirates.

As disturbing as it is to imagine, I have come to see that if I had been raised in my grandparents' home, just as my father was, I might not have done any better. I can't be sure. That uncertainty is jolting. It was through meditation that Hanh came to more deeply understand the humanity of the pirate.

For me, it was the act of volunteering and then subsequently working in domestic violence programs and also teaching about violence that have served as a sort of guided meditation. It was in working with violent men and in teaching about their tactics and strategies that some of my dad's behavior that at once felt confusing, lonely, and scary began to make sense and have meaning.

I once learned from a gardener that a "volunteer" is a plant that grows independently from a seed that was not deliberately sown, though once it appears, it may be encouraged to grow by people tending to it. I did not get into domestic violence work totally consciously; it just felt like the right thing to do when I was twenty-one. It was a practical, albeit naive, application and extension of my work in gender studies. Of course, I soon learned that it was really a practical application and extension of my own life.

Similarly, my dad had no idea—and neither did I at the time—that what he was doing all those years when he was cruel and then kind and then cruel again would water and fertilize the seed from which I would grow into committing my whole life to antiviolence work. I see now that my dad's decision not to pursue that volunteering job at the shelter after all was because he would not have been able to truly volunteer in a way that would have cultivated his and others' growth. He started thinking about volunteering there in a way that was not at all organic. I think that had he continued, he would have been regarded as an unwanted, overgrown weed in that half-alive garden of survivor women walking a labyrinth of fear and hope, searching for rootedness. Did his idea to volunteer, and then his decision not to, stem from what he saw violence do to his mother? To my mother? To me? He never chose to carefully examine his behavior and the effect he had on other people. I think if he had, and if he had softened years earlier, the way he did in certain moments at the very end of his life in the nursing home when he spoke with me about his mother and my mother, he might have been able to truly be a volunteer, to ally with others, and to live out his own life and finally till the filthy soil of his past with a love that could have stretched him more deeply.

The problem is that my father had no idea what to do with these generations of damaged crops that were passed down to him from his father and probably his grandfather and great-grandfather. Without a son to whom to hand down this metaphorical farm, he gave this legacy of abuse to me, his daughter, and it was from this scorched family landscape that I chose to reinvent what my life gave me.

One morning as I write, I'm reminded of a favorite poem by Naomi Shibab Nye titled "Valentine for Ernest Mann," a piece that reminds me time and again that we have to live out our lives in a way that also helps us reinvent our lives:

You can't order a poem like you order a taco.
Walk up to the counter, say, "I'll take two"
and expect it to be handed back to you
on a shiny plate.

Still, I like your spirit.
Anyone who says, "Here's my address,
write me a poem," deserves something in reply.
So I'll tell a secret instead:
poems hide. In the bottoms of our shoes,
they are sleeping. They are the shadows
drifting across our ceilings the moment
before we wake up. What we have to do
is live in a way that lets us find them.

Once I knew a man who gave his wife
two skunks for a valentine.
He couldn't understand why she was crying.
"I thought they had such beautiful eyes."
And he was serious. He was a serious man
who lived in a serious way. Nothing was ugly
just because the world said so. He really
liked those skunks. So he re-invented them
as valentines and they became beautiful.
At least, to him. And the poems that had been hiding
in the eyes of skunks for centuries
crawled out and curled up at his feet.

Maybe if we re-invent whatever our lives give us
we find poems. Check your garage, the odd sock
in your drawer, the person you almost like, but not quite.
And let me know.

Three summers before my dad died, he came to me in a dream. Crying, he said, "Oh, I wish I treated those years with so much more love." It's as though grace had finally made its way toward me, more generously than ever before. Perhaps this was the poem I had so often longed to find, to write into being, this story that's far more complicated than whether abusers know they abused, regret what they've done, and can change. It's more of a legacy, of how we learn love and, ultimately, what we do with it.

11

Random Acts of Kindness

Sometimes I am jolted awake, even midday, by the nice things my dad did for me. So I thought I should make a list:

1. I was always afraid of rodents, almost paralyzingly so; I still am. When I was in school, I was unable to read books that had pictures of mice. My dad always went through the books and taped index cards over the photographs so I wouldn't be afraid and so I could do my work. I recently received an Oprah magazine that contained a photo of a white mouse with a pink tail, and I nearly dropped the magazine on the floor and couldn't read the article. I thought of my dad and what he would have done for me.
2. He collected all my diplomas and had them all matted and framed.
3. He regularly made trips to Pincus Bakery for rugelach, special cookies, and rye bread that my friend Emily and her family adored and remembered from when they lived in Cleveland, and he schlepped to the post office to ship the treats to them. He bubble-wrapped everything, as though he was wrapping expensive glassware, so nothing would even crack or crumble and spent a fortune on sending those packages.

4. He taught me how to ride a bike, and then when I was fifteen years old, he and I were driving home from a Saturday of doing some errands, and he said, "Okay, you're going to learn to drive today," and he took me to the parking lot at what was then Byron Junior High School and let me try out the car. It was exhilarating, and it's something my mother never let me do. Ever. She still refuses to drive with me, and she has never let me borrow her car.

5. He took me to a rink to practice how to roller skate so I would be able to attend Betsy's birthday party when I was ten without being embarrassed or having to sit it out.

6. He took me alone on road trips to look at colleges, since my mother thought it was perfectly pointless to look at a bunch of buildings.

7. When I needed to find housing in Austin, Texas, he traveled with me to look for an apartment. At one of the complexes, we were out by the pool, and he accidentally took a step backward and fell in. He emerged from the water laughing, exclaiming, "Wow, that was really refreshing."

8. Later, when I was frantically trying to finish my MA degree in Texas and planning to move to Massachusetts to continue my PhD, he went by himself to Boston to find me housing and made a deposit on a place for me.

9. He took me and my friends to amusement parks every summer, rode the rickety roller coasters, and crashed into us in the dodgem cars despite having a bad back and bad knees.

10. Every winter, he took me to Thornton Park to go sled riding, and the best was when he got down on his stomach and then let me lay on top of him on my stomach, and we flew down the hill at breakneck speed, even when he knew his back would kill him the next day.

11. He let me stay up late so we could play Boggle for hours. He always wanted me to have a great vocabulary and to spell well.

12. Every Valentine's Day, he shipped me bags of milk chocolate hearts wrapped in red foil.

13. He left work early to attend all of my school events and assemblies, and he went in late after dropping me at school so I wouldn't have to walk the four blocks, since even then I disliked early mornings. When I came home from college, he left work to meet me for long lunches. This was the 1970s and 1980s, when fathers were far less present and involved. My friend Lisa's mother always described him as more like a mother hen.

14. After screaming at me or my mom and calling us disgusting names and threatening to do horrible stuff or getting beet red, raising his fists, gritting his teeth, and seething, a few hours later, or usually less, he'd come to my bedroom, kneel at the side of my bed, hold my head, caress my face, and tell me how sorry he was, how it would never happen again, and he'd kiss me goodnight.

It's crazy, but I think I looked forward to the apologies.

12

Death Notice

When my dad died, I opted not to have a death notice or obituary published in the *Plain Dealer*. I figured, if there was no funeral, what use was a blurb in the newspaper? The people I wanted to know about his death would learn it from me, and anything else seemed unnecessary. A death notice also seemed like a set of statements that would only imbue his life with more loneliness, since I would be the only person listed as surviving him, who cared about him, with whom there was a relationship that had outlived his life. I did not want to draw attention to that.

But people do indeed read obituaries, especially older people, and it is a way for the deceased to say, "I lived. See? This is what I did. I was in the world. I made a difference. I mattered. Here's the list of the people who will really care that I am no longer going to be around. Life is short, so stop reading these words and rush out and go live your life."

After all this time, I figure I should finally write something.

DEATH NOTICE, VERSION #1:

James S. Cohan, eighty-four, of North Royalton, died Monday, August 13, 2012, at Regal Care Nursing Home.

DEATH NOTICE, VERSION #2:

James S. Cohan, eighty-four, not really of North Royalton, only living in a nursing home there because the other ones shipped him out for bad behavior, died Monday, August 13, 2012. Actually lived in Shaker and then Beachwood.

DEATH NOTICE, VERSION #3:

James S. Cohan, eighty-four, not really of North Royalton, only living in a nursing home there because the other ones had shipped him out for bad behavior, died Monday, August 13, 2012. Actually lived in Shaker and then Beachwood. Almost died twenty-five years earlier from an operation for an aortic aneurysm, and then almost died again seventeen years after that from hip surgery because his heart was suspected to be too weak to make it through the operation.

DEATH NOTICE, VERSION #4:

James S. Cohan, eighty-four, not really of North Royalton, only living in a nursing home there because the other ones had shipped him out for bad behavior, died Monday, August 13, 2012. Actually lived in Shaker and then Beachwood. Almost died twenty-five years earlier from an operation for an aortic aneurysm, and then almost died again seventeen years after that from hip surgery because his heart was suspected to be too weak to make it through the operation. Could have also died from any of the other following health issues he had endured for years: a heart attack, complications from diabetes, and kidney failure.

DEATH NOTICE, VERSION #5:

James S. Cohan, eighty-four, not really of North Royalton, only living in a nursing home there because the other ones had shipped him out for bad behavior, died Monday, August 13,

2012. Actually lived in Shaker and then Beachwood. Almost died twenty-five years earlier from an operation for an aortic aneurysm, and then almost died again seventeen years after that from hip surgery because his heart was suspected to be too weak to make it through the operation. Could have also died from any of the other following health issues he had endured for years: a heart attack, complications from diabetes, and kidney failure. Actually did die many times over, in his daughter Deborah's mind.

13

Obituary

James (Jim) S. Cohan died, maybe not so peacefully, of congestive heart failure in North Royalton, Ohio, on Monday, August 13, 2012. He was eighty-four. He died alone, with no one around except an aide he barely knew who had given him dinner about an hour beforehand. He died without saying a word that whole day. He was born in Newark, New Jersey, on September 29, 1927, to Bertha (née Rappaport) and Jack Cohan. He had one sister. Her name is Absentia. He was married to a woman in the early 1950s. They had a couple of kids and divorced in 1959. He remarried in 1967 to a woman named Naomi Marks. Together they had one daughter, Deborah, and after separating in 1999, they were divorced in early 2000. Naomi was the love of his life, but he didn't always treat her that way. They made another go of it in 2001 for less than two months. Like most sequels, this one really sucked. In fact, it totally bombed.

Cohan graduated from the S.I. Newhouse School of Public Communications at Syracuse University, where he was one of the five founders of the college radio station and was on the swim team. For more than twenty years, he worked as an executive vice president at a major advertising firm in Cleveland, Ohio. Prior to that, he was vice president of another advertising agency and before that was vice president of advertising for a large supermarket chain. He probably wished he had gotten to be president of all these companies. In the early part of his career, he lived and worked in New York City and then in Columbus, Ohio, and then moved to Cleveland, Ohio, in 1967, where he lived until his death. Cleveland was a city in which he lived more than half his life yet claimed to despise because of its dreary weather. He longed to live in the south or southwest, where it always appeared to be sunny and warm.

Cohan had no real hobbies, which was a problem in his marriage to Naomi, and he often left her to do things by herself. He adored photography and should have pursued it even more than he did. He had an unusually good eye for great design; was a decent golfer when he played, which was seldom; loved good food so much he should have been a food critic; was a brilliant writer; and planned and dreamed of trips he never went on. He became involved in politics when volunteering for the John Kerry campaign.

Having been raised much more religiously than he liked, he rejected religion as an adult and was not affiliated with any synagogue. He identified as agnostic because he found the label of "atheist" too harsh and severe.

Cohan was known to be an incredible speller; he participated five times in the *Plain Dealer*'s Corporate Bees for Literacy to benefit Project: LEARN. His spelling talent goes far back; when he was a child, his family staged spelling bees for the kids and gave out small prizes. When he did his homework and needed help with a word, he knew better than to ask his parents and instead familiarized himself with the dictionary.

He is survived by one person, his daughter, Deborah. She and her ex-husband did not have any children, so there are no grandchildren or great-grandchildren. Having not spoken to his sister and her children in decades, it would be hard to say Cohan is survived by them. Rather, he is survived by silence and blank space. He had a few friends, but they stopped calling and visiting over the years. Because of his lack of relationships, there will be no funeral service, no memorial service, no vigil, no graveside service, no visitation, and definitely no sitting shiva. Deborah will arrange to get her own bagels and cream cheese, and anyway, what good is a shiva if she hates noodle kugels, casseroles, blintzes, and most of all, leftovers of any kind? Traditional shivas seem to be about making grief even more intolerable; urged to sit on uncomfortable stools low to the ground, mourners are not supposed to shave or wear makeup or work or bathe for pleasure or have sex or listen to music or do anything joyous. But surviving years of grief before a death is hard enough, so what's the harm in doing all that stuff?

The Ohio Cremation Society will make ashes out of Cohan's body, and the ashes will go in an urn in the ground in a cemetery no one he knows has ever even seen because it was the cheapest place to go.

For further information, please don't call Deborah because she will finally be turning off her phone after thirteen years of crazy phone calls. Donations may be made in Cohan's memory to paying back Deborah's student loans or to the therapist she saw for years. No, that's tawdry. Fine, to the American Heart Association. No, they get a lot of donations, and anyway, he had too many health problems to pick just one organization. That wouldn't be fair to the American Diabetes Association, or the Kidney Foundation, or any of the others. You could donate to the University of Wisconsin–Madison, where Deborah went because Cohan had stated in his will that if for some reason he outlived her, he wanted his money to go there. Ah, you know what? Forget it, keep the money. Use it on a trip to somewhere tropical that he would have loved or splurge on a once-in-a-lifetime dinner at an extravagant place. And by all means, make his death, and my grief, less lonely and toast to him.

14

Ashes

"Hi, Debbie. I am sorry to tell you, your dad just died." The call I had long anguished about was really happening, right there at 5:50 p.m. in the airport in Savannah, Georgia. For years, I had wondered how much more time we had left, wondered where I would be when I got the call. I never could have imagined that I would be on my way to visit my father that same night, scheduled to arrive in Cleveland at 11:46 p.m. Upon hearing the news, I fell to the floor crying. The ticket agents approached, asked how they could help, if I indeed wanted to still get on the 7:12 p.m. flight as planned or if I wanted to be rescheduled for a later time. I didn't even stop to think about it. I knew I would not fly out. I knew I just needed to head back to my house in South Carolina, the state I had only lived in a month at that point. There would be no funeral. Who would come? My dad's so-called friends and former colleagues had not come to the nursing home to visit him in years; a few other friends had died. Some of the friends from his marriage to my mom stayed in her camp. I knew that my Cleveland friends would be there if I wanted them, but really, I knew I would prefer to get together over sushi and coffee, not have a reunion at a graveside. Anyway, my dad was going to be cremated, and there was no way I was going to fly by myself to the Ohio Cremation Society to see my father's dead body.

Before I mustered the energy to make the drive back across state lines, I figured I should pull myself together over a cup of tea in the airport and make some necessary calls. Disoriented, I wandered to the tables near the Starbucks and dumped my bags on a chair and the floor. I walked over to the coffee bar to place my order, and a couple of women were ordering vanilla lattes, the teenagers with them ordering caramel Frappuccinos, and I thought, "Can't you see something really big happened today? I just lost my dad!" My tiny world had frozen, yet it seemed everything and everyone around me was frantically, dizzily, maniacally spinning. I wonder how many times I have been out, going about my life, in frenetic motion, when I have, without even knowing it, encountered people in their loneliest hours, at the edge of their deepest fears.

I took my tea, sat down, and pulled out a legal pad and my phone. I called the nursing home back, this time a bit more composed than when they called me with the news, and they told me, "Your dad's body will be picked up around 8:30 p.m." Okay, not exactly the chauffeur service that he would have most enjoyed, but fine. I thought back through all the years I wished I could have picked him up myself to take him out to a great dinner, to a movie, to something, anything. But doing so would have required hiring an aide, with money we ran out of years ago when my father went on Medicaid. Even with adult diapers on, wearing stained shirts and sweatpants, he still had visions of going to the cool restaurants in Cleveland. I did what I could to bring him dinners I thought he would like—ribs from Damon's; huge, extralean corned beef sandwiches from Jack's Deli; calzones from Pizzazz; and shrimp with black bean sauce from Shuhei. But I still sat there at the airport feeling like I had come up short, like he deserved better outings, that he should have been picked up and taken out more.

Next, I called the man at the cremation society. The funeral director there offered to send me my dad's ashes. He said he could FedEx them and that they would arrive within a day at my front door. I did everything I could to not yell back, "You've got to be fucking kidding me!" The thing is, my dad never got to South Carolina. He dreamed of the Carolinas as a place to retire, since they sounded beautiful to him, but he never actually went. And he never got to see my house. I didn't think receiving his ashes in my brand-new home would be the best way to invite him in for the first time. I never even got to have him over for a home-cooked meal, since we have always lived miles apart, and when he came to Boston to see me, he always wanted to go out to eat in all the best new restaurants. I mean, what would I do if my father's ashes were delivered to my house—pick him up off the front mat at the door and stick him on a chair at the dining room table in front of a placement, maybe with a place card that reads "Dad"? When I explained that I preferred that the ashes be buried in the ground, the funeral director told me that I could send anything I wanted to be included in the urn before they buried it. My friend Pat suggested that I make jewelry that could store his ashes. I knew she meant well, but I really couldn't see myself wearing my dad. I decided to send pictures instead.

My instinct was to send a lot of stuff for this last send-off. I had a zillion photos I wanted to include in the urn. My mother remarked, "What are you *doing*, preparing King Tut's tomb?" I guess I just didn't want my father to be so alone. However, I was not sure how best to send photos for an urn. Does one include a letter or some sort of gift? Every year on his birthday or for Father's Day, I asked my dad what he wanted, and he would always say, "All I want is a kiss and a card." But this time I royally fucked up. I never made it to Cleveland before he died to kiss him goodbye; I missed that by six hours. And I couldn't even get it together to write a final card. What I was trying to do getting this package together started to feel so cheesy, so contrived—there didn't really seem to be a need for a note. Instead, I went back to that day he so often described, November 17, 1969, the day I was born, before I possessed language, before we exchanged words.

He always wanted to have the last word. I felt then that he should have it. It was only fair. After all, he *died*. I figured I would get my final say in writing about him—not in a vengeful way, I hoped, just in a way that would make meaning. So I sent only pictures. It's the way we started this life together. In that nursery at Mount Sinai Hospital in Cleveland, he relentlessly, shamelessly took all these pictures of me. It is through that lens, through that framing, that he began to see our world together, to envision it, and to build it, with my mother, for me. For the three of us, this tiny, strong, yet fragile family.

I sent photos of the family we once were, pictures of my mother, Mark, and me. I anguished about putting the pictures in the best order as though a sequence actually mattered underground. I kept copies of the pictures I sent. I see that in most of these childhood photos, I look very pensive, very solemn, perhaps disturbingly so—as though a very contemplative adult face got pasted to a child's playful body. There is the one of me studying the water when I was about three years old, looking like I am searching for something. There is the one of me on a train with my mother seated behind me, both of us gazing out the window, longing for something. I now wonder what that little girl saw, what that little girl wanted so badly. There is the picture of me, almost three years old, standing beside my father, who is seated on a plastic outdoor chair with his head slightly bent over so we are about the same height. We're leaning into each other, adding colored blocks to some large thing we are building, trusting we will construct it carefully so it won't topple over.

In the envelope of photos I sent was the black-and-white one of my dad at my wedding to Mark, in which he is holding a camera, taking his own pictures, meticulously documenting the day. You can see him behind the Nikon, grinning approvingly on this most age-old, conventional sort of occasion. Less than eighteen months later, he broke his hip and would never stand unassisted again or hold a camera to take a picture. The pictures he took at the wedding were the last pictures I ever saw him take. The picture of him at the wedding is the last photograph I have of him in any semblance of what I would call well. I can't count the pictures taken of him by the nursing home staff for the Christmas newsletter when he was in a wheelchair, donning rubber gloves, peeling carrots for a cooking activity of beef stew. I don't think I had ever seen my dad peel a carrot or make a stew. This version of my father just wasn't the dad I knew.

At the nursing home, the staff had older pictures of the residents, from when they were in their prime, posted on the doors to their rooms. Even with that reminder of how they used to be, I looked at some of the residents who seemed the worst off, especially the woman who could barely keep her head up and squawked in an irritating high-pitched voice like a sick bird while seated with my dad at dinner, unable to imagine her any way but this way. It was an unfair rendering. I knew this, and yet I still couldn't reconcile the sad vestiges of humanity in the nursing home with the younger images posted on their doors. I wanted to scream to anyone who would listen, "This is my dad now, but lemme tell you what he used to be like!"

My father adored his precious Nikon camera. He even wanted it at the nursing home. Somehow, he still wanted to take pictures. I think he believed he would eventually leave that hellhole. He begged for me to send him his Nikon. I kept putting it off. Mark, being as frugal and cautious as he is, insisted that sending my father his camera was crazy and urged me not to ship it. He insisted it would break or be stolen. In some ways, he seemed right; it seemed like the most unnecessary thing to have lying around a nursing home. But at some point, I remember thinking, if this is what my father wants, he should have it. A few weeks before I told Mark I wanted a divorce, I drove from Boston to Cleveland by myself to see my dad and bring the camera. This was the same camera my mom had lugged around for him on trips. She always shied away from the camera and never used it to take photos herself. Even with his picture taking, I did not grow up with family portraits around the house; in fact, there was not a single framed photo of all of us together. Instead, my mother neatly mounted every picture on black paper in scrapbooks and in white pen recorded every event with creative titles and dates. I am sure my love for photography and documentary film grew out of these rituals.

As soon as I moved to Bluffton, one of the first things I did was set out to find an old-fashioned photo-finishing place. I brought them pictures to develop that I had been taking for two years on my favorite walking path in Wellesley, Massachusetts. It was on that path winding around Lake Waban that I worked out in my head my need for a divorce, where I plotted out writing projects and job applications, and where I anticipated my life without my dad. I had the shop make ten 8 × 10″ photographs. I took them to an art framer and had them each matted in white with black metal frames. I carried them to the car and sank into the seat crying, thinking, "Wow, my dad would have loved to see these."

In the urn are his ashes and also some fragments of his vision, of a little girl, looking outward yet inward, confused yet clear, precocious yet small, holding those blocks saying, "Let's make things!" The truth is, I still want my dad around to see my new life, the one I've been building all by myself. My dad was with me at the beginning of my life, taking pictures. I am at the end of his with pictures. And therein lies the age-old story—that if life works as it is supposed to, where children outlive their parents, then our parents know our story, our narrative, from the day we were born. Parents know our past, our present, and can anticipate our future. As children, we come in to the middle of the movie. We are with our parents as they age and die. We missed their beginnings. They will miss our endings. It's the ending I want him to see, to know.

Before I licked the envelope with the photos inside, I took one last look at the picture of my dad in the eye of two cameras, the one taking a picture of him taking a picture. I stared lovingly and I whispered to it, "Keep watching me, Dad. In fact, look at me now. Quick, because it's all about to change."

My dad awaited cremation while wrapped in cold white bed sheets in a cardboard box and was finally cremated on Saturday, August 18, 2012. I thought that cremation was a quick process; I had no idea it would take hours. According to traditional Jewish law, cremation is forbidden, and I assume that Saturday then, being the Sabbath, is the number one day to not be cremated. But I am just glad his wish for cremation was fulfilled, since at one point a few years back, I was told it would be too expensive. Or as Mark used to joke, "It's the way to go if you have money to burn." The funeral director attempted to assure me that there would be no confusion as to whose body it was before or after cremation. He explained that a metal disk was attached to the outside of the box so it wouldn't get burned in the process and that a small laminated tag with all of my dad's identifying information hung outside of the cremation machine. I kept asking myself in disbelief, "So this is how it all ends up?" I tried to find some comfort in my dad's urn being buried in the ground in a cemetery I have never seen and may never go to. I have never really understood people going to "visit" people at cemeteries.

Once the cremation was over, one of the directors of the cremation society emailed me the message below with an accompanying set of photos of my dad's urn and grave, and these became the last pictures I have of him:

Deb,

Please see attached the photos of the marble urn, which your father was interred in. Also see the urn placed in the grave and, finally, a photo orienting you as to the section of the cemetery he is in.

In the final photo, the grave is filled in, but if you imagine the photo divided into quadrants, the grave could be seen in the middle-left portion of the lower-right quadrant.

I hope this is helpful.

Thank you.

It was through this process that I began to understand my dad being in and of the earth. The first big life event that I had to endure after my dad's death was his birthday. This happened six weeks after he died, when he would have been eighty-five years old. He shared a birthday with a little girl named Nayelis who died at the age of three from cancer, just a few months before my dad died. Her mom, my friend Yvette, was a favorite former student of mine, and we've stayed in touch for many years. After Nayelis died, Yvette requested that everyone release balloons to honor and remember her on what should have been her fourth birthday. It seemed like the least I could do, and I also intuited that this would somehow be a catharsis for me also. So in the afternoon of Saturday, September 29, I stopped at Kroger for two huge balloons, one that read "I love you" for my dad and one with Hello Kitty for Nayelis, and drove to Coligny Beach to release them. As I walked onto the beach, I spotted a little girl, ironically no more than four years old, and she looked curious and excited about my balloons. It seemed perfect to share this moment with a child, and so I proceeded to ask her parents if I could invite her to join me in releasing the Hello Kitty balloon and if they would take pictures of this. The mother said, "Oh, but I don't want her to get sand in her shoes." "But it's a fucking beach," I thought. So instead, I wound up releasing both balloons alone, and the father took pictures of me doing this.

I have always been obsessed with death, worrying about when it will happen, who will die first and how. I really just want to understand what remains. Still, hurtling toward fifty, I don't have a will. Without kids or any really significant assets, I haven't gotten around to making one. Yet I am consumed with what will happen to me when I am very old, maybe too old to care for myself, or if something happens much sooner, whether I will just suddenly get sick and die. One of my young colleagues, who was just about thirty, died suddenly at the end of one of the first semesters I was teaching at the university, and I remember that I immediately texted Kim, my work wife, that I am putting her in charge of being sure there's a blowout party if I, too, suddenly drop dead. She agreed and said that she also wants a festive party when she dies.

But beyond the party, I am worried about the ashes. I know I want to be cremated, and when I was married to Mark, he knew, and also teased me, about my elaborate plans for what he was to do with my ashes. I explained that I wanted them divided into thirds—one-third going to Madison, Wisconsin, a place that was formative to my very being, to my becoming a feminist, a sociologist, a writer, a creative soul. It's where I went to college, and it still feels like home. I wanted another third of the ashes going to Hawaii, since that is where Mark and I spent our honeymoon and our birthdays together—the one when I turned forty and he turned fifty and I joked that we were having our ninetieth birthday. I wanted Mark to hold onto the other third to disperse in places he thought I would like to see that I never got to see. I was never sure whether he would really comply with my wishes. It would be foolish to say that's part of why I wanted a divorce, but in some ways, it is sort of true. I worried that if I got sick, he wouldn't do what was needed or would leave me feeling very much alone. He wasn't the sort of husband who on his way home wondered if I needed anything or surprised me with something I might want. Our marriage wasn't filled with a lot of emotional extras. He tired easily, and I worried that if I was sick, he would say he didn't have the energy to do or get or make whatever was needed.

Seven months after I met Mike, I broke my finger in a hand mixer making red velvet cupcakes for a colleague's retirement party. I already had a hysterectomy scheduled two weeks later, but when I broke my finger, the surgeon told me it was a very bad break and that I would need surgery right away. He sent me down to the nurse to talk about all the pre-op procedures, and in the moment, I panicked. I did not have a ride to and from surgery, and I hate asking for help. I was not sure how I was going to manage by myself. I had never had surgery in my life, and now was about to have two in two weeks. I asked the nurse if I could make a quick phone call to see if Mike could take time off to help me. In a reassuring way completely characteristic of him, he said, "Let me see what I can do." And within minutes, he got back to me and said that his coworker would change a few of her vacation days and that he would stay with me. Every three hours, he woke up to slice bananas and to give them to me with graham crackers or saltines so I would have something in my stomach as I took the painkillers. Looking back, I guess I was a complete pain in the ass. At 1:00 a.m. and 4:00 a.m., I insisted he had messed up, that he was giving me the wrong drug at the wrong time. I think if I had said that to Mark, his response would have been, "Fine, Deb, then do it yourself. I'm exhausted. I'm going to bed." And I would have likely felt even more alone. Mike tried to explain that he had sorted and counted it all out properly before bed and laughed and then said to me with the slightest southern drawl on the word damn, "Deborah, just take the damn pills."

The month prior to that, my bladder stopped working. I found myself at Mike's suddenly unable to pee. I realized it was probably that my uterine fibroids had gotten too large and were pressing on my bladder. I felt like my body was submerged in urine that would not come out, that eventually, it would spring forth from my head. Mike said, "I know what makes me pee." "Yeah, okay, what?" I said. "Beer." And he poured me a small glass of beer. I drank a little and still nothing happened. He started Googling about what to do. No matter what, I could not pee. I knew something was very wrong, and he took me to the emergency room, where they inserted a catheter that had to remain inside me for four days. Before we left, I asked the nurse for bed pads, since I was worried the catheter would somehow leak urine on Mike's bed. Later, I told a few friends, "Hey, you know a guy is a keeper if he will sleep with you in his bed while you are wearing a catheter, lying on bed padding and still find you attractive. And if the next day, when he realizes you packed only shorts and pants for this weekend getaway and realizes you'll need a skirt or dress to get through days with a catheter, he will take you shopping. And then if he takes you out for brunch at a favorite local place and then to a marina to watch boats go by, just to help take your nervous mind off your body, keep him around. And when that same man sleeps next to you for eight weeks post-hysterectomy and knows that you absolutely can't have fingers, a penis, a tongue—I mean *anything*—inserted into your vagina and somehow still makes you come from just kissing and touching, by all means, keep him. Hold him tight."

Mike and I are not married. In fact, I'm almost a hundred percent certain we will never get married. I know he doesn't want to, and I suppose I am not sure I truly want to be married either. Yet I find myself wanting Mike to be my husband. Most of the time, I feel like he already is and so I refer to him as such. We have the arrangement I always joked was better for marriage anyway—living in two separate houses. To be fair, since we met, we have lived two hours apart because of our jobs. The thing for me is this—I want the experience of marrying someone I am as in love with as I am with Mike.

Mike has been married before, twice in fact, and from the people I know who have been married and divorced twice, there's a feeling of failure in the marriage department, maybe even more of a rejection of the thought that marriage is a viable thing to do. Mike and I often see people getting married at the beaches near our homes, and when the party looks lavish and expensive, held at one of the resorts, Mike insists it must be a first marriage. He says, "It's a good thing they're getting the first one out of the way while they're young so they can get in a few more later." Or "Hey, look, they're starting to fill up their marriage stamp card. Pretty soon, they can get a free sandwich."

Without being married, I suppose I can't really ask or expect Mike to be in charge of my ashes. Anyway, he's ten years older than I am and once told me while we were sitting on a bench overlooking the May River that he thinks he will die when he is sixty-eight. I have no idea where he got this number from and neither does he. Perhaps it's that as a small child, he watched as his dad died of a heart attack in the bathroom; or maybe it's that he can't imagine his life without running and assumes he won't be able to run marathons in his seventies, eighties, and nineties; or maybe it's that unlike me, he is simply not that interested in growing extremely old.

I still think sixty-eight years old is awfully young to die these days. Surely that does not give me enough time with this man. I am a little envious of his ex-wives, who got the extra time with him, but then I am also glad we met later on. I needed to wrestle with marriage first. And I am still glad I married Mark. The advantage to meeting the love of your life in your forties and fifties and not in your twenties and thirties is that the essence of what matters comes into fuller focus. There's so much stuff in life not worth worrying about, and we're not so hell-bent on being right.

While I worry about ethereal stuff like what is going to happen to my ashes and who is going to remember me, when it comes to aging, Mike seems solely focused on the practical day-to-day issues, like who will wipe his butt when he's weak and dying. He once said the first marriage is the starter marriage, the one on training wheels, to just get people in the swing of marriage; the second marriage is to become miserable; and the third one is to guarantee you'll have someone around to wipe your ass. According to his calculations and marital assessment, since he has been married twice and I have been married once, he could get ass wiping from me, but then I would be miserable. But actually, I don't think I'll ever be miserable with him. I now understand those couples who, if one gets brutally ill, the other one claims to want him or her around however long is possible regardless of what is involved. I will take Mike however I can have him.

If I die first, I still think Mike would be the best person to handle my ashes. He works in public relations and is an expert in crisis communications. He would write the perfect press release about my death. However, I am also positive that if I die first, he will easily get a new woman to love. He's hot and totally unassuming about it, and most importantly, as my mom pointed out after seeing a picture of him before ever meeting him, he looks like he has a warm and generous spirit.

One night at dinner, I finally shared with Mike my concern about what would happen to my ashes after my death. He said, "Oh, no problem, I'll put you in the closet with Casey." Casey was his beloved golden retriever who died some months before we met. He keeps Casey's ashes in his front hall closet.

"But that's the problem. I don't want to be stuffed in a closet; I want to go places, see things."

"But you'll be dead, so you won't see anything."

"Just put me in a container and stick me in the glove compartment, and when you go places you think I'd like, just bring me out to explore and have fun." I live my life trying to be everywhere, do everything. I think I want a death ritual that extends this.

As he put more dressing on his salad and buttered his baked potato, he said, "You want to hear a funny story about ashes?" And he went on to tell me about how when he was married the second time, he and his wife went to her family's summer home in Beaufort with her mother and sister and sister's family. The sister's family had just lost their dog, Harry, and had a ceremony by the banks of the river to remember him. The problem was that when Mike's sister-in-law went to throw the ashes, she forgot about the direction the wind was blowing, and Mike wound up with Harry's ashes all over him and up his nose.

Days later, I was reading an essay by Elinor Lipman, who, in reflecting on her husband's remains, says that she knew there would be "no sprinkling or parting with the only thing we had left. Ashes are sadder than I ever could have imagined." And then I suddenly questioned myself—perhaps I have made too much light out of this ashes thing, tried to make this unbearable process, dare I say, fun. Maybe there is something to hanging onto ashes, never letting them go. I don't have any regrets about my decision regarding my dad's ashes, but I plan to handle it differently with Mike. If he dies first, I will keep him. If he decides he wants me to scatter his ashes over the bodies of water that he adores, I will, but I'm sure I will hold back some, trying to keep as much of him as I can for myself. And if I die first, well, I want to be dust dancing around a moonlit sky, but at the same time, I secretly hope that Mike will know to keep a portion of the remains of me just for himself. I think I'm really just trying to tell him, "Don't ever let me *completely* go. Take me out and play with me always. Remember me. God, most of all, remember *us*."

15

Birthday Letter

Dear Dad,

It's Monday, September 29, 2014, your eighty-seventh
birthday. I would normally call you in the morning and
sing "Happy Birthday" to you in the worst singing voice
ever. As you know, there's a good reason my music teacher
had me learn sign language rather than sing for our
performances in elementary school.

Today, Erica called to let me know she was thinking
of you and left a voice mail saying that, in your honor, we
should really be having one of our "dictionary calls," as she
refers to them now. Remember when she and I were little
and you couldn't understand how we always had so much
to talk about every night on the phone, and so once you got
on the line and said, "What are you two doing? Reading
each other the dictionary?" It stuck. You stuck. When you
died, she even had a picture made of a dictionary with a
huge letter *A* to suggest that with our busy lives, we can
barely get past *A* when we talk, so we will always have
things to talk about. It's framed and hangs in my office at
school. I see you in that picture.

And this morning, I got a message from Mark telling me he was thinking about you too. He's really a mensch. And, Dad, I found a new mensch, this time in the form of a nice Catholic boy. His name is Mike. You'd like him. A lot. Most of all, you'd approve of how he cares for me. Just last week, he took the whole week off work to be with me as I was recovering. See, I had to have both ovaries removed. It was emergency surgery, because one of them got twisted, and it was horribly painful. I thought of you in the emergency room last Sunday when they weren't sure what was wrong with me. I thought of you because I was scared and figured you would do what you could to make it okay. The doctor claimed I had a fibroid uterus that was giving me trouble. I looked him straight in the eye and explained that I had my uterus removed last July in that same hospital. You would have laughed, since you could never stand the arrogance of some doctors. You always remarked how some people didn't know their ass from their elbow. Well, this guy didn't know an ovary from a uterus. But, Dad, I feel so old now. I can't believe that I am now officially menopausal and on a hormonal patch. Aging is so strange. You taught me this when you were alive, and you helped me see it as you were dying, but I didn't get it until recently.

We were both born on Mondays, so our birthdays fall on the same day every year. I was at the grocery store recently buying half and half for the Starbucks coffee I still drink every day and chose the one with my birthday as the expiration date. Three weeks ago, I bought yogurts and chose only the ones with your birthday as the expiration date, as though our special dates would bring me good luck, would bring you back.

The thing is, Dad, I see you everywhere—in crab cakes, in pretzel rods, in Bombay martinis straight up with colossal olives, in roasted brussels sprouts, the dish du jour in every classy restaurant. Too bad you got sick and died before this vegetable became so in vogue and before I learned to love them too. I see you in pictures of decadent dishes at restaurants, in brochures of swanky boutique hotels, in great logos and slogans you would have celebrated, and in bad journalism that would have pissed you off. I see your intolerance for irrationality when I interact with unbearably stupid people who cannot function without enforcing everything annoyingly bureaucratic. I try to be more patient than you were, but it ticks me off also, and I see you. I see you in swimming pools; in framed black-and-white, dramatic photographs; in catalogs of well-designed, modern furniture; and in advertisements for new performances at the theater.

When I'm listening to my Spotify playlist and Ray Charles suddenly comes on shuffle and starts singing "You Are My Sunshine," I see you. The first time I heard that song after you died, I was watching that movie *Trouble with the Curve*, and I wept by myself in the theater. The next time I heard it, I was standing in Mike's kitchen because he was playing it for me, having no idea what it already meant to me, and I burst into tears, my face turning red and blotchy, and everything I mumbled was inaudible. I wanted so badly to listen to the song and enjoy it, but at the time, it just stung too much, felt too raw. I desperately wanted the music on, yet I desperately wanted it off. Mike offered to turn it off, not wanting to see me so sad. I said no. I wanted to see you.

Occasionally, when Mike sends me his daily morning emails, he addresses the message, "Good Morning Sunshine." I don't think he knows this, but it helps me see you. I also see you in that Paul Simon song you introduced me to when you spoke at my wedding with Mark, "Father and Daughter." That one I can't bear to add to my playlist. I use my iPhone in the car and when I walk for exercise, and

I think if that song were on there, I would either drive into a telephone pole or walk into a tree. But when it comes on the radio, I see you. Or sometimes, I purposely play that CD at home so I can see you.

Over the summer, when Mike and I toured Fenway Park, we saw glimpses of luxurious loges, and I remembered all those times we sat in those together watching games and eating snacks and getting to meet cool people, and so I saw you. When I extended the expiration date on the frequent flyer miles with United Airlines and had to log in as you, I thought of all the places you would have loved to travel, and so all I could do was see you. The webpage even said, quite eerily, "Welcome, Mr. James Cohan." I see you when I am grading student papers, and so much of the writing is sloppy and hard to read, and you see that I am commenting nonstop. You tell me to just go have fun and enjoy my life. I see you at the beach; and on golf courses; and when I order smoked salmon, sliced cucumbers, red onion, and tomatoes on toasted everything bagels slathered with scallion cream cheese at a favorite café in Savannah. Sometimes I see you when Mike makes a joke with insanely perfect timing or does wordplay or says a pun, and when I tell Mom about some of these funny lines, she laughs and remarks, "It's like Jim Cohan rises again." Even she sees you. We see you.

When my friends post on Facebook wanting prayers for their parents having surgeries or struggling with dementia and they need to move them to a dedicated facility, I see you. When people post on Facebook wishing their fathers a happy birthday, I see you. When they post that their dads are having eighty-eighth birthdays and beyond, I see you, and then I get really jealous. When I was quoted in a prominent publication for saying something about a case involving a football player and domestic violence, I see you. Not because of the violence, surprisingly, but because you would have bought a hundred copies of the paper and handed them out, saying, "This is my kid."

I'm writing this book about what it meant to me to care for my ill and elderly parent against the backdrop of complicated family dynamics. That sounds so academic— abstract and ridiculous. That description is the ten-second elevator speech to sum it up. But really, I'm writing a book about you, about me, about us, about how the *you* you were shaped the *me* I am. You'd hate parts of the book, I am convinced of that. Some stuff would piss you off. Or maybe it would make you sad or regretful. You might say, "Deb, how dare you tell everyone this or that?" However, this book is the only liberating thing that came out of the fact that you died. You can't read my work and edit it. Deep down, though, I somehow believe that even if you could read the book and edit it, strangely, you might not, because in it, you'd see me. See a different side of me, a resilience borne of your resilience. And you would leave it be. And maybe you'd get it, and you'd get me in a whole new way. You might also read it as the love story that it is. Because there's no way I could have sat here all these months and written all these words without all this love—this crazy, deep, conflicted, magnetic, wild, outrageous, huge love. When I returned to school this fall, people asked how my summer was. I wanted to say, "Well, I spent most days with my dead father." But I couldn't say that. That would have sounded really weird and would have made everyone uncomfortable. But it's the truth.

I've spent these days with you. Because I see you in all there is.

I love you so very much. Xoxo.

Doodles

16

Relearning to Fly

Steve Martin and the Steep Canyon Rangers have a song that goes, "Go away, stop, turn around, come back. Go away, stop, come back." It's about wanting a lover to both stay and go; to be here with us, but not too close; to leave and give us space, but not too much space. This seems to be the paradox that exists in every relationship, not just romantic ones. And for most of my life, I didn't seem to know how to get it right, to find that balance.

For me, this tension seems most evident at the airport. There are the arrivals and departures, the connects and disconnects, the gates and the terminals, the rushes, the delays, the flights, the crashes, the soaring, the descents, the welcome hugs, the farewell embraces, the chance meetings, and the deliberate encounters. When I first set off for graduate school in sociology, I thought an interesting research project would be to do an ethnography of airports. Many years later, I see that I really don't need to formally conduct a study on airports to learn something about human relationships or the human condition. Without knowing it, or even trying, I had accumulated much of what I needed to understand about love, loss, hope, and fear at Cleveland Hopkins, at Boston Logan, at Savannah, and at the Charleston airports.

It was Christmas Day 2004 that my dad fell on the ice and broke his hip at Cleveland Hopkins; it was at Boston Logan that I began to feel the rumblings of my marriage on the precipice of crashing; it was at the Savannah airport on August 13, 2012, that I got the news my dad had died; and it was at the Charleston airport where Mike dropped me off to catch a plane so I could attend a writing workshop that I relearned how to fly.

By the time I met Mike, the airport had become a dreaded place for me, packed with fear, overbooked with loss. I had been to the Savannah airport twice since I had moved to South Carolina—once to drop off my mother on August 1, 2012, after she helped me move, and then twelve days later, on August 13, I was right back there, standing at the ticket counter to check in to my flight to Cleveland to say goodbye to my dad one last time, when I got the phone call that he had just died. Up until August, that airport felt filled with promise and a sense of the future. It's where I was picked up and dropped off for my job interview at the university. When I left the Savannah airport to head back to Boston after the interview, I was filled with the excitement of what was to come. Soon after that, the Savannah airport became a place of loss, where I said goodbye to parents and to my life as I knew it.

When I went to visit my dad in 2002 before he got so sick, he picked me up at the airport. He drove up and approached the cashier to pay for parking on our way out, and I could see that the attendant was preoccupied doing what looked like homework for school. I anticipated my dad's impatience, worried that he would believe she was not focused enough on him. I was impatient myself, wishing there was a way to communicate to her, figuring that I would somehow later pay for his being ticked off with having to wait. I wanted to say, "Come on, lady, pay attention—my dad's in line. He's not patient; he'll tear your head off if you don't respond to him instantly. But Jesus Christ, I have to be with him for another week, so hurry up, will you, before he tears *my* heart out?" One of the things about witnessing and experiencing abuse for so long is that you often start to take it on before it has even happened. That's part of what it means to walk on eggshells. Knowing what my dad was capable of made me afraid and anxious in that moment with a stranger, a cashier who had done nothing wrong, and with a father who also had not yet done anything wrong. What usually resulted from situations like this was that my father accused me of being edgy. The truth is, of course, that I was edgy, but who wouldn't be? He had no understanding of how his behavior produced my reaction. But I think my hypervigilance was about operating under an illusion that I would have the power to prevent trouble before it happened, because the voices that are hauntingly torturous are the ones that say, "If only you had done this, or if only you hadn't done that, he wouldn't have done whatever it was."

Later that evening, when we got back to my father's apartment, he dropped me off in the garage. I took my suitcase out of the trunk and proceeded to go to the guest suite on the first floor of the building where I would be staying for the week. I desperately needed to use the bathroom; the last time I had gone was hours and hours earlier at the airport in Boston. Apparently, the door of the suite locked behind me. Minutes later, there was insistent knocking on the door. My father stood there accusing me of being "selfish" and asking, "Couldn't you have waited to use the bathroom? You knew I was parking the car and coming to your door, Deb." It wasn't exactly a warm welcome home. And yet the crazy part was how, for months, he had begged me to visit, claiming he couldn't wait to have me home.

For years, my dad had been used to monitoring my comings and goings; ultimately, he became a man incapable of even knowing what year it was, a man soon unable to tell time, finally handing over to Mark the Rolex watch that had been given to him upon his retirement from decades of overwork. And then rather than enjoy it, Mark, being as austere as he is, kept it in the safe deposit box, only taking it out to wear on certain special occasions.

By the time my mother left my father, my dad had more plans of moving on than he was actually able to carry out. He was a man connected to the idea of being on the move but not always doing what was needed to get going. Nowhere was this more painful to witness than when I cleaned out his apartment and found a relatively new yet empty passport. This same sense of being stuck had also been permeating my marriage. Mark was working just a little more than part time, not actively job searching, and spending endless hours in front of the television. Trips with Mark often left me feeling lonely as well. There were times we were waiting at the gate for a plane and I had to use the bathroom. I would ask him to watch my bags, but he wanted me to take them with me. It seemed to be too much of a bother for him to wait with my stuff until I came back. And as we'd wait for the plane, he never wanted to talk or be silly or play a game together. And when I actually did have to take trips alone, either for an academic conference, an interview, a writing workshop, or a retreat or to see my dad or friends, he made a big production over dropping me off and picking me up at the airport, but not in a good way. Sometimes he said he'd take me and then threaten to renege, or he'd want me to take the Logan Express Bus, or when he finally did just drive me, which is always what happened in the end anyway, he put up a stink about where to pick me up at the airport. When he'd drop me off, he always worried first about the car and how it was illegally parked, so he was reluctant to engage in a long hug and kiss goodbye. When he'd come to pick me up, he'd focus on the luggage first, grabbing that before grabbing me, and he'd get in the car, and I'd turn to try to hug and kiss him. I dreamed of a different kind of greeting. I became sad when I would see other couples reuniting at the airport—lovers who had gone away from each other, turned around, and come back. For too long, our relationship was stuck on the tarmac.

The first time I had to pick up Mike at the Savannah airport when he returned from seeing his family in Dallas for Christmas, we met at the security checkpoint because it was as close as I could get to the gate, and he looked as happy to see me as I felt inside seeing him. He grabbed me, nuzzled into me, and murmured, "Mmmmmm." And one time Mike drove me to the Charleston airport so I could take a plane to Provincetown, Massachusetts, for a writing workshop. I figured he would just drop me off at departures, but he had planned to park the car and wait with me. I told him it wasn't necessary, so he wound up leaving the car illegally parked at the curb and helped me bring in my bags, then kissed and hugged me near the ticket counter. So of course I felt terribly guilty when a week later he came to meet me in Boston and he took the Logan Express Bus out to Braintree so we wouldn't be caught in rush hour traffic on a Friday. I suggested to him that maybe I should drive from Provincetown to Logan to pick him up, feeling all too aware of how comings and goings had been handled in my marriage and not wanting to reproduce any of that. I knew I was susceptible to reproducing familiar behavior patterns, even unwanted ones. For example, at the hotel on the day we packed to come home, Mike remarked that I looked like a whirling dervish. I was used to having to be that way when I went to the airport with my dad or with Mark, who were sticklers about being early. On the flight home when we were delayed for hours, Mike and I sat at the airport and ate sushi, meandered around, and people-watched, and he made silly jokes. What I learned with Mike was how easy and fun and happy travel—and the comings and goings—could be. For years, I had been mired in relationships with men—my dad, Mark, and other men I had dated—that had me consumed with feeling so stuck and with what it would take to get unstuck.

In the nursing home, my dad had his eye on one of the fancy red motorized wheelchairs used by a few of the other men there, and yet he also asked me about renewing his driver's license. He always wanted to be in the driver's seat. He either wanted to be living back in his own home, driving his own nice car, or wanted to know he'd have the Mercedes of wheelchairs if he was going to be stuck in one. And I wanted all this for him but had no means to buy it. He asked me, "You don't think I'm going to be like this the rest of my life, do you, Deb?" I would reply, "No, of course not, Dad. I hope not." It was a lie bundled around a whole lot of hopelessness, but I had to convey it as hopefulness. It was one of the hardest parts of caregiving—seeing how my father longed for previous dimensions of his life and simultaneously anticipated the future with more hope than it would ever bring forth and then feeling compelled to just go along with his far-reaching fantasies. Those were the moments when I could most keenly see and feel what he—what we—had lost and how much loss was really still to come.

My visits back and forth from Boston to Cleveland to see my father became a series of steps—going away, stopping, turning around, and coming back. There was ambivalence in my relationship with my father because of his history of abuse, and that ambivalence got particularly accentuated in caregiving. Every visit when I arrived, I almost instantly wanted to leave, to get out of the narrow hell that had become our lives. And then on the day I had to leave him and say goodbye to come home, I wanted nothing more than to stay, because I feared it would be the last time I would ever see him. The day I left, I was flooded with a thousand things I suddenly wanted to tell him or ask him. But during the visit, we just stared at each other, my head exploding with how to cram in and ask all these questions, how to show that much love, how to let him go without showing him he was dying. In fact, I usually got outside of his room, or down the hall, or near the revolving door, and went back for one more hug, one more kiss, one more time to tell him how much I loved him. He'd ask me if I had stuff to read at the airport in case my flight was delayed, and I always replied, "Yeah, I have a lot of grading." I was what I had so desperately wanted to become—a professor—yet underneath it all, at the core, was a woman morphed back into a little girl just wanting her daddy.

In the summer of 2009, Mark and I decided to drive to Cleveland to see my dad. He called to ask when we would be arriving. It was a good ten-hour drive, and I didn't want to be pinned down to a specific arrival time. We were supposed to get there on July 1, but I lied and said July 2 to strategize around his impatience. Abuse diminishes integrity—for everyone involved. I didn't want my dad to expect us earlier and get impatient and angry if we were late, asking, "Where have you been?" as though I was fifteen years old again, out with my friends beyond the time he wanted me back home. In that same phone call, he told me he wanted to buy a tan-colored suit from a fancy store on Fairmount Boulevard. I asked why he needed it, and he told me he would be walking the next week and wanted to wear the suit out to a nice place. Of course, he hadn't been able to walk in years and would never walk again. All I could do was to learn to say, "Sure, Dad, we can go there when I am home."

We lived for years with this unrealistic rendering of what he was capable of doing. Like the time when the nursing home threw a big summer party with a car show, a magician, animal-shaped balloons, and a cotton candy machine, and I saw my dad staring at the toilet he said he needed to get to—and badly—yet there was no way he could make it on his own. And in the same moment, he went on to tell me how much he looked forward to leaving the nursing home and playing golf soon. This was the same weekend we tried to play word scramble games—games that for most of his life he would have beaten anyone in, and he just couldn't do them.

There was the other time when I told him I was teaching a few classes at Harvard and he literally fell asleep; if he had been well, every person in the home and beyond would have heard that his daughter was teaching at Harvard. This incident actually made me want to cry and laugh hysterically all at the same time; there was no one in the world that had ever beamed with more pride at these sorts of accomplishments of mine, and it killed me to think he could not even process this news anymore. And at the same time, it was hilarious. I mean, who had ever fallen asleep when I said Harvard? The people who saw that on my vita always commented on it. To be honest, I didn't really care to talk about Harvard. Everyone's awe made me uneasy, since there were other places I had actually enjoyed teaching much more, places where I had mentored equally bright students or brighter. But these were the moments I knew he was really sick, slipping further and further away, not stopping, not turning around from those crazy places of incontinence both in his body and in his mind, not coming back.

People believe that if you grew up witnessing and experiencing abuse, you will likely be doomed in future intimate relationships. When I moved to South Carolina by myself, even I began to believe that too. I had just divorced and wondered if maybe the love story I was looking for was just not going to be part of my life narrative, that other great things could and would happen in my life, but maybe not love exploding across the pages. After my first date with Mike, though, he asked more about my writing, so I sent him a chapter of this book. When we talked about it on the phone, he tried to say that he wasn't like my father, that he had never been abusive, and that he wished there was some sort of way to make certain that I knew this. Of course, having worked with abusive men in the past, I knew how easy it could be for a man to say this to a woman with whom he wanted to be intimate, to distance himself from anything bad or scary that too many men do. And I had seen enough women friends fall prey to this sort of thing.

But there was something about how Mike said it, something in his voice, something in my bones that knew this was not some sort of manipulative stunt to convince me but was real, genuine, and pure, something I could trust. It was so early in getting to know him—we had emailed and phoned for almost a month before we met, and we had only been on one date. Granted, our first date lasted about eleven hours, but still. I think I trusted more than just his word that he wasn't violent. I trusted the process of putting all my information out there for him to know about me and then seeing what he would do with it. I trusted how he would receive it. If I had heard this story from a friend or colleague, I would be telling her to be very careful, to not share information that made her so vulnerable so soon. It's hard to explain how I knew that this time it was okay, that it wouldn't set me up for an abusive relationship, that Mike wouldn't use this information against me or criticize me with it later, that my heart would be safe. It would be held just tightly enough to show me great love and loosely enough to give me space.

Navigating between the tight spaces and the looseness is necessary in our relationship, since we live two hours apart.

The tight spaces can't be just when we are together and the loose times when we're apart. We have to make stitches in the fabric of our relationship every day that we aren't together for the loose times to feel connected and whole, and we need to give each other breathing space and looseness for the stretches of time that we're back together. This is what finally allows love to explode across the pages of my life. This elusive narrative of love is finally something I can call mine. Mike and I always have to go away from each other, stop, turn around, and come back, again and again. And doing that over and over and over finally makes it so I, so we, can fly.

17

The Birth(day) Ring

During the years I cared for my dad, my mom's absence felt like a death. Though she is very much alive and I talk to her regularly, my mother wasn't part of our tiny family in the same way anymore. Often, I was asked by the medical professionals caring for my dad where my mom was, if she had died. It was similar to when friends in college asked me if my parents were divorced, though it wasn't until seven years after I graduated from college that they actually split up. I had always talked about my parents separately and had different relationships with each of them, so in many ways, it made sense that people assumed my family was in fragments.

When my mother left the marriage, I began to understand divorce as a sort of death. It's the death of a family unit, a structure, a way of being, a way of having a self in the world. So much needed to be reconfigured physically and reimagined psychically.

I got my next hard lesson in divorce as death when Mark and I split up in 2010. I cared about Mark and still do, but nothing in our world was set up to make sense of, or to support, two people who had great love for each other but could no longer make their marriage work. This divorce was even more foreign to people since Mark and I did not have kids, so we actually made a conscious choice to stay connected.

In February 2011, I was in the greeting card aisle in CVS looking at Valentine's Day cards when I was confronted with three rather contradictory realities. First, Valentine's Day had always been my favorite holiday after my birthday. Next, after celebrating Valentine's Day with the same person for fifteen years, I became aware that it would officially suck that year and for probably many years following, since I was now single again. Finally, it was impossible to find an appropriate Valentine for one's ex-husband, even in this day and age of "congratulations on your divorce" cards that are designed for women to send to each other in a mail/male liberation party of sorts.

Sure, Valentine's Day is the ultimate manifestation of the commercialization of intimacy, the quintessential formulaic holiday. But it doesn't matter. I love Valentine's Day because I'm passionate about every shade of red and hot pink, all things chocolate, and uninhibited expressions of love and desire. I'm comfortable telling people I adore that I actually adore them. In junior high and high school, we had carnation sales, and I longed to be the girl with the biggest bouquet; we all wanted that, so we sent flowers to each other, and I think some of us secretly wanted to send them to ourselves to be sure we got even more.

For me, divorce was an excruciating process but an unusually simple event. On December 21, 2010, Mark and I joined millions of couples the world over when we gave our marriage a vote of "no confidence." We stood before a judge with our attorneys in between us, in boy, boy, girl, girl order, and we recited to the judge what he wanted to hear. I wore a hot-pink V-necked cashmere sweater, maybe four shades lighter than the electric-pink silk dress I wore to our wedding on June 29, 2003.

I stood there, in that cavernous room in the Cambridge court where my attorney told me that the only happy thing that happens there are the adoptions, and I looked left at Mark, wondering what was going through his mind, and then I stared out the window, aware of what was going through mine. In my mind, I heard him speaking to me on that steamy day in June in front of eighty-nine of our closest family and friends as he said, "I promise to be with you through all the changes in your life." I still believe he probably will be, though now it is from afar, for we decided to divorce with a certain sense of love and care. So much so that when Erica, my friend since well before carnation days in junior high, asked me how it all went in court, I explained that we drove to court together and went out for soup and coffee afterward. She said, "Of course you did!" Our wedding was not typical, so it was fitting that our divorce would not be either. The way we went about crafting our wedding with artistry and feminism and color both troubled and intrigued people, and it turns out that our split produced the same response—both the breakup itself and the way we chose to handle it.

When I began to tell my friends we were divorcing, I suddenly had compassion for my mother, who, upon sharing with friends about her divorce from my dad, encountered a bizarre set of responses and learned how much the news of divorce makes others come unhinged, unraveled. One friend even told me that she was sure her husband thought divorce was contagious, since a bunch of their friends were doing it, and he was worried it would happen to them.

People seem invested in divorcing couples hating each other. It is much easier for the onlooker if they have a clear sense of who to root for, and I have started to think it might even be easier for the people involved. We live in a world in which it is hard to hold two opposing experiences together and embrace each of them; the comparing, judging mind doesn't allow for that. Divorcing with love and compassion poses an important challenge—we must hold the experiences of connection and disconnection and touch the tenderness and tensions of both.

One very dear friend shared with me her mother's response to our divorce, saying, "I told my mom about you and Mark, and she said, 'No shit.'" Nothing was surprising to her about our breakup, though her response made me realize something profound. Divorce is the death of a family we chose to create and the disruption of a circle outside ourselves. Who in their right mind would exclaim "No shit" upon hearing about the death of a friend's loved one? It would be too cruel.

The most meaningful response I got to the news of my divorce came from an unlikely source. Betsy is an old, dear friend from when we were five years old. But I wrongly assumed her life experience would color her ability to say anything helpful. This is a friend whose mother died suddenly when we were in first grade, and she has devoted her entire being to marriage and motherhood; both are sacred callings for her. She was one of the last people I told because others' responses made me hesitant to tell more people, and I worried about telling people in Cleveland anyway. It always felt like an emotionally incestuous place where gossip traveled faster than the speed of light. But after Betsy told me she thought I was one of the strongest people she knew and that she was confident I would make it through that emotionally trying time, she went on to say, "You know, marriage is a tall order; it's a lot to ask of people to stay together for their whole lives." No response to my news was more astute and more honest. I didn't assume that because she was able to articulate that sentiment, it meant she and her husband were experiencing problems. I saw it as a gracious gift of friendship that she was able to exist outside of herself and to be with me in that moment of total impermanence.

I realized my ongoing affection for Mark when we went through our house, methodically deciding how to split up our stuff, and somewhere in the midst of it, in the kitchen, he grabbed me and tickled me, and even as I clung to the legal pad with the sharp line down the middle and the words "Deb's Stuff" on the left and "Mark's Stuff" on the right, I also clung to him, to a sense of us, and to the me that for so long made sense to me in our marriage. I burst out giggling, and we hugged. The saddest part of that story as I see it now is that he never tickled me or reached out to play that much during our marriage. And then, as would be expected given the task at hand, we proceeded to argue about candlesticks and napkin rings and glass bowls and vases and frames and all the other stuff that made up what we all want to call home. And I got angry when he wanted the patio furniture, the luggage, and the treadmill, since all that stuff symbolized leisure and going places. But since I was planning to move across the country and he was staying in the house, it made sense to leave some of these things behind. I knew the marriage meant something to him when he fought me on so many wedding gifts, asking me, "Why are you getting to keep all our nice gifts from our friends? I want nice things to remember this too."

During our divorce proceedings, we lied to the judge. We said I would be moving out within forty-one days. At the time, I did not yet have a new job and was looking all around the country for work. I really did not want to have to move twice—once to move out of the house and once more for a new tenure-track faculty position at a college or university somewhere. And anyway, Mark needed the money that I would be giving him by continuing to split the household expenses. So even after divorcing in December 2010, I did not move out of our house until July 15, 2012. This means we lived together through three wedding anniversaries while broken up.

Immediately after our divorce, Mark shoveled my car out from every harsh winter storm and continued to do the laundry, making sure I had clean underwear—something I still believe is crucial to find in a live-in partner. And before every interview out of state, he called to wish me good luck. I helped him write cover letters as he looked for new work and proofread important documents for him. Occasionally, I cooked some of our favorite meals, and we rented movies together. We even continued to sleep in the same bed, since we only had one bed in the house, though we had sworn off sex and any sort of fooling around. During those years, we occasionally gave each other a hug or held hands, but those gestures didn't carry passion as much as they carried care. And they carried the weight of a history together and a completely uncertain future. In that house that we had built together, in that relationship that we had built together, were two single people trying to feel less alone. In some ways, those days weren't that much different from when we were married. Of course, that was the problem.

I had a husband who loved me and who I loved. I now have an ex-husband who still loves me whom I still love. The texture and flavor of the love had to change, of course, but it's still a kind of love. In the folds of the years, in the crevices of memories, there's this love. It's the sort of love you have for someone when you've done something together, so basic to the human condition, so conventional and yet so radical, this joining hands and deciding to say to each other and to the world, "We're in this together, for life." For me, the marriage didn't end with a shortage of love. It ended because I didn't feel like I could grow or we could grow well together. I couldn't stay like that, in quite that form, but the love remained, in a new, blended way.

I think grief first fragments the self, and then it does something to integrate the self. Grief rips at us, tears at us, splinters us, leaves too much of our life in shards, and threatens to make us absolutely insane. And then grief dares us toward wholeness, to coming to forge a new way.

In November 2012, my mom came to visit me for Thanksgiving and for my first birthday in South Carolina after my move. On the morning of my birthday, right after breakfast, I excused myself from the table and went to my desk. I wanted to be with my father, even for just a few minutes. So I grabbed the cassette tape that contained the recording of a phone message my dad had left for me on my fortieth birthday, a message in which he sang to me and told me how happy he was to be my father. I took the tape recorder and the tape, sat down on the floor of my walk-in closet, and played my dad's message. His voice always sounded decades younger than it was, and I listened to him wish me a happy birthday, bringing him into my day as best I could. We always had a family tradition of celebrating birthdays in the morning, so it seemed fitting to hear his voice early on that day. I didn't tell my mom what I had been doing. She had no way to know I had already done what I could to have my dad with me that day.

It wasn't the first time I had gone to a closet to find and get closer to a parent. In December 1999, when I went to Cleveland to help my dad move out of our family home and into his apartment, I found myself wanting my mother, wishing she were there. Badly. It felt eerie and wrong for just the two of us to dismantle the house. That was the first time my family felt dead. I went to her closet then, and though it was empty of her clothes, it still had the plastic hanging wardrobe bags, some with mothballs inside. I sat on the tan painted wooden ledge at the very back of the closet, a place where I had sometimes hidden as a child or at other times just sat there as she tried on different outfits and I kept her company. So in the midst of this excruciating move, I retreated to the closet, hoping to find a space to be with her, even if just in my mind.

As a little girl, I sat on that ledge in the closet longing to be all grown up. It was like sitting on the toilet seat or the edge of the sink, as so many little girls do the world over, perched to get the best glimpse of our mothers, applying makeup, getting ready to go out. My mom's routine was minimal as she wore little makeup, nothing more than some blush and a mixture of usually about three lipsticks. Gypsy-like in appearance, my mom rarely needed more to intensify or exoticize her look.

My mother possesses an outsider look. She embodies all that is unusual. She looks artsy, funky, bold, and intriguing. As a little girl, I wanted a mom who wore more conventional stuff, maybe argyle or cable-knit sweaters, or a Fair Isle pullover with a Henley neckline, so common in the 1980s, or a preppy look with Lilly Pulitzer's pink and green frogs leaping across the fabric. But that wasn't my mom. And now I am glad that she wasn't run-of-the-mill. She had various hair clips for the ponytail that she wore as I was growing up, and I watched her put those on, something I could never do since I always had shorter hair. Whatever my mother lacked in an intricate makeup and hair routine, she made up for in jewelry. I always loved my mother's jewelry, loved trying it on and loved watching her choose the bracelets, necklaces, and rings she would wear each day and on special evenings when she would go out with my father. Perhaps as little girls, as some of us load up our faces with our mothers' makeup to try to look grown up or try on their jewelry, their hats, and their shoes, we are really just trying to get as much of our mothers as possible.

This book, then, is a story of access—of how I had too much access to my dad; of how maybe I have craved more access to my exceedingly private mother, sometimes hard to reach or hard to understand; of how maybe the birth of a baby makes the intimacy of a marriage harder to access for many couples; of how a divorce makes parents harder to access, even for adult children; of how caregiving for an ill parent gives us access to things we might not even want and renders other things less accessible; of how divorce makes everything accessible and inaccessible all at once; of how death makes everything accessible and inaccessible all at once; of how we look to objects and places, like cassette tapes and closets and jewelry to provide new and different access to those we miss; of how in the end, maybe nothing really provides access to what we seek. Maybe it's only the outrageously long, crooked path of grief that eventually gives us access to greater knowledge of our past, awareness of our future, and reflection about ourselves. It's that path of grief that I walked through my parents' divorce, my divorce from Mark, my dad's long illness, and ultimately his death.

On that night of my birthday, my mom and I returned home from dinner, and she gave me my presents. I hadn't wanted to open them right away in the morning as was typical in our family and preferred to save them. A tradition of my mother's had always been to give me either a new silver bracelet or one that had belonged to her, a painting she had made, and maybe another fun, frivolous thing or some sort of big wow thing. On this birthday, she had arranged to have two new pieces of artwork Federal Expressed to my house in gigantic boxes. They were gorgeous—vivid, geometric, vibrant, architectural new prints she had just made and had framed, and I was excited to hang them immediately. Then she gave me a bangle that had once been hers that I adored.

And then she brought out the gift that was supposed to be *the* gift that year.

It was in the tiniest box. I couldn't imagine what it was. I opened it and found a ring, one she wore almost every day of my youth and even occasionally in more recent years. It was yellow gold, a metal neither of us usually gravitates to since we both prefer silver. I was confused to see the ring, in a box, being given to me, no longer on her finger. I didn't understand why she wanted to part with the ring, why she wanted me to have it.

She explained to me the story of the ring, that a few weeks before I was born, she and my father were at a beautiful store in Cleveland, and she spotted the ring and loved it. When she was in the hospital, my father left to buy the ring, to present it to her right after I was born. They always affectionately referred to it as the "Debbie ring." The ring is twisty, loopy, and overlapping in ways that echo the concentric circles and enmeshment in our tiny family.

Suddenly seeing the very object that my dad had gotten my mom forty-three years earlier was jarring and only made me miss him more. And it made me want to run far from my mother, far from the only family member I had access to. I said to her very quietly and calmly but with such distress and emptiness, "Mom, I can't wear this," and I immediately gave it back to her. I felt I was holding something I should not have, at least not yet. In receiving that ring, it felt like once again, I was left alone with too much of my father. There had been so many times my mother felt like the odd person out, too many times my father's domineering ways relegated her to the sidelines of our relationship and she felt rejected, too many times I intentionally and unintentionally sided with him. She had always remarked how hard it was to have a family of three.

Rejecting her gift created a rift between us, one that we were unable to mend during that visit. She was angry. She was sad. And I was angry, and I was sad. In the moment, the gift hit me like one more death. It hit us both like a huge rejection, but for entirely different reasons. Neither of us understood what the other one actually wanted and didn't want, and we were left wanting something the other could not give.

To me, in the moment, the offering of the ring felt like too much and too little—the symbolism was too loaded, too hot, too much to hold onto, and yet there was also too little left of this family that once was. Being given the ring that had held my parents together at such a new, tender, challenging time—the birth of a baby—that also signaled and celebrated the birth of a family was too much to bear. It's weird. I finally got access and then didn't want it.

I saw my mother's offer of the ring as a parting gift, like she was really done with that family of ours. I felt left alone, asked to wear the memory of my birth and the memory of a family that was born when I was and existed until a third of it had just died. When she gave me the ring, it was a reminder of what I had felt during all those years of caring for my dad. It felt like she had already died, that they had died as a couple, and that we had completely and totally died as a family. And as it was, I already felt that I was too much of my dad's life, and when she gave me the ring that he had given to her, it felt like she was rejecting her role as a wife or a mother all over again.

I needed and wanted to see her wearing the ring, hanging on to the memory of our family too, not giving it away. But I see now that this would have been too much to ask of her. I would have been asking her to still feel the love of that family we had created so long ago, to wear a ring just to assure me it wouldn't all die. Perhaps my anger and sadness was my own projection, not wanting an important relationship in my life to be gone. Now I understand what she was trying to do. She saw this gift as a way to bring my father back to me for that messy first birthday after his death. Of course, there was nothing she could do, nothing that would bring my dead dad back.

Perhaps in giving me this ring from the early days of her love for my dad and his for her, she was giving to me a symbol of what I had grown to understand about my relationship with Mark—she was giving me a love, and a sense of family, in an entirely new, blended way, acknowledging me as an adult woman, with all the grown-up things I had been doing for my father, finally birthing myself.

18

The Worry Machine

Grief teaches.
—Kay Redfield Jamison

I am an expert worrier. I could have gotten a PhD in it much sooner than it took me to finish a doctorate in sociology. I have perfected worrying, made it into a high art. I worry about things that have happened, I worry about things that will happen, I worry about things that might happen, and I worry about things that will never happen. I even worry that I worry too much. In first grade, my teacher said, "Turn off the worry machine." It's a nice idea, but it's like my ex-husband, Mark, telling me in the most noncomforting way, "Just relax," when even he, too, seemed tense. Advice like this just leaves me worried about how to truly relax.

As an only child, I spent most of my life worried that my parents would die. Who would die first, when would it happen, how would it happen? Some of this worry stems from my own irrationality about death and dying. And it is also about how fully I am living my life and whether I am squeezing every drop and savoring it perfectly. I think it's all also part of my quest to live a life that makes death complete something it cannot. The Buddhist writer and teacher Pema

Chödrön inspires me, as she writes about impermanence and the power in seeing that worrying about things changing is its own ultimate death. She says that real living is about constantly being thrown out of the nest, living a life that is always topsy-turvy, and being open to that instability, showing loving kindness to yourself in that process. She insists that anything else is death. One day, I hope I fully reach that way of thinking, actually embodying it, living it out, making it mine. Until then, I worry that I have a very long way to go.

In my thirties I was in therapy, and the therapist had me visualize what I looked like to myself when I was in intense worry mode. I remember that I closed my eyes, and in less than a minute, an image came to me. Dancing around frenetically in my mind was a picture of one of those pencils that was popular in the eighties, which I sometimes still see around, that had colorful, crazy, soft hair where the eraser would be, and if you took the pencil and rolled it and rubbed it really fast in your palms, the friction made the hair stick out everywhere. That's what I have come to see as worry—it's heat, it's friction, it's mind motion. It propels us, yet often it paralyzes us. It's my mind on fire. In therapy, I came to call this image "Pencil Person." That's how I must look in those maniacal moments: scattered and crazy, all over the place, but a bit stuck. This Pencil Person still likes to hang out too much, like an uninvited guest, just lingering, annoyingly. I have tried to befriend her or at least laugh a little when I think of her.

When my dad died, it was like Pencil Person wanted to establish permanent residence in my head. I very immediately started relentlessly worrying chiefly about two things: (1) that my mom would die and (2) if I would ever again meet a man who would be open to try to understand my family. Now, remember, I was raised an upper-middle-class Jewish girl from Shaker Heights, Ohio. I'm very liberal, a feminist with a PhD, and a college professor. This doesn't exactly make for effortless matchmaking in Bluffton, South Carolina.

The day after my dad died, I called Mark to let him know, and I said, "Thank you for knowing my dad. Actually *knowing* him." I think I was really saying, "Thanks for accepting and loving him—and me—anyway." Despite the issues in my marriage to Mark, he had a capacity to show love and concern for my parents and for me amid all our shortcomings. When I married Mark, I was glad that he met everyone that was important to me in my tiny family—my mom, my dad, and my grandma, my mom's mom. I wished he could have met my grandpa, but he had died when I was thirteen. Mark knew my grandma and my dad and hung out with them and had fun with them before illnesses set in and robbed them of who they had been. With my dad, he went to Indians and Cavs games, saw *Riverdance* and came home trying to imitate the moves, went to the fireworks at Shaker Middle School, devoured gigantic steaks and onion straws, went to Sea World and concerts at Blossom Music Center, and meandered through different cities. And with my grandma, he went with me to pick her up to take her to lunch at her favorite restaurants, he talked with her over tea and homemade meringue cookies and handmade chocolate-dipped fruit in her dining room, and he sat with me as I interviewed her so I would always have her accounts on film after she died. It rattled me to think that because I was divorced and my dad had just died, the only person left for a man to meet would be my mom. It felt so partial, so incomplete. Not because my mom isn't enough. In actuality, she could account for about half a dozen people given the size of her personality. But meeting just one person in a family felt like it was not enough.

Given my dad's private rages and public humiliation rituals, I was also somewhat relieved to know that whatever new man would show up in my life would get to escape his scrutiny, his wrath, his scathing character assassinations, and the way he tried to punch holes in other men's masculinity. Even though not having him around meant simultaneously losing out on his humor, his wit, his wisdom, and his fun. Without knowing the full cast of characters in my family story, though, I worried that this person wouldn't ever be able to grasp the whole story and thus truly know and understand me.

My mind works like this: it spins an awful storyline that I can't stop. For example, my mother will die. When she dies, I will no longer have any family alive with whom I am in touch. I will have no one to ask about my childhood or give me information about my family. *When my mother dies, I will be left with no family.* The statement overwhelms me in its starkness, its absoluteness. I will be completely alone. I do not have siblings, a husband, or children. I have bought into the cultural narrative about how a large family could provide protective coating during the most profound moments of my grief. I have Mike though. I assume I still will, at least I hope so, when something eventually happens to my mother, though what if he dies? I have friends, many, many old, dear friends. I have always said my friends are like my family. Maybe that was a lifelong defense mechanism I installed early on to deal with the fear of being left without blood-related family. One day, I will be tested, to see if it's really true—that without blood-related family, friends are family enough. Whatever happens, when my mom dies, I will not have the mental guardrail that having a parent can provide.

Here are some of the most important big and little things you should probably know about my mother. First, picture Iris Apfel, the ninety-eight-year-old designer and fashionista, and you have my mother, complete with the nearly identical, epic, oversized glasses in various colors. I've watched the documentary *Iris*, and it was like listening to my mother's musings about art, the creative process, and nonconformity. Both are eccentric, opinionated as hell, colorful, dramatic, and vibrant. My mother though has a steely desire for privacy and is exceedingly stubborn, not trusting, and rigid with everything and everyone, and as she ages, she possesses an odd combination of free spirit and panic-stricken caution. She's fully impossible and yet fully lovable. She and my father certainly had *that* in common.

When I was in kindergarten, my mother baked chocolate cupcakes with rich buttercream frosting and then made flags attached to toothpicks to put on top with each child's name in my class. A highly accomplished artist, she nonetheless has trouble telling the gallery owners when we meander the streets of Boston that she has paintings and prints to show and sell, ones that would look fabulous in their space. She buys cases of frozen mangoes at Market Basket so she's ready to make a smoothie almost every night, the sound of the blender driving the men she has lived with absolutely crazy. She loves to blast John Denver and Neil Diamond when she paints, and she adores Johnny Cash. When she had to have an MRI, they asked if she wanted any music to drown out that dreadful jackhammer noise, and she asked for Bruce Springsteen. When those artists come on the radio or on my iPod, I immediately think of her. I wonder what will happen when she dies. Will I ever be able to see straight when I look at art or hear music? Or will I go completely crazy? And I can't go anywhere with her for more than about seven minutes without someone commenting on her huge, bold, bright-red glasses, her trademark, the ones framing her sculpted face, with its high cheekbones, enormous brown eyes, and a now balding head. Her hair loss is not from cancer; she has some ridiculously rare, stupid, autoimmune skin disorder, and hair loss is a side effect. She has a sense of humor about it though.

She tells the hairdresser, "You're good with scalp." Everyone has always remarked how spunky, energetic, and gorgeously dramatic she looks. They're right; she does. But on our last few visits, her pace has slowed down when we walk, and I find myself impatiently sad about my aging mother. It's like Pencil Person has intruded on our visits.

"It's almost like you're taking it out on her that she's aging," Erica points out to me as we are talking on our phones in our cars, she in Cleveland waiting for her daughter to finish a dance lesson and me dashing off to the chiropractor. There's nothing like a lifelong friend from childhood to hold up a magnifying mirror to the pimples on our personality. It's just that as my mom slows down, I notice that her aging looks more sped up. I find myself wanting to say to the universe, "No, stop, no, not another parent, not yet." Losing one parent was obviously hard, but anticipating that I will eventually lose another one feels much harder. I think that losing the first parent begins the most primal story of attachment and loss; losing the second one seems to amplify and finalize that story.

I have long been obsessed with my parents' aging. I remember being in the backseat of my dad's luxurious chocolate-brown Buick with the plush tan suede-like seats and the wood paneling. The car felt enormous to my little-girl self. I imagined that I could grow up and even live in it one day. I would sit in the middle of the back seat and lean all the way in with my arms slung over the front seat, inching close to my parents up there, always wanting to be privy to their adult conversations, and one day, I blurted out, "You know what? When I am forty-five, you will be eighty, Mom, and, Dad, oh my god, you will be almost ninety!" And when I said this, I was only about eleven, and so my mom was about forty-five, and my dad was about fifty-three. It all seemed outrageously far off and crazy to even think about. And now, as I write this, we are past these age markers. The calculations feel different now. In some ways, eighty-something doesn't sound as old anymore because it's my mother. I listen as she tells me about her friends just recently diagnosed with various, hideous forms of cancer, and I hear the sad worry in her voice. And she also tells me about her friend who is doing amazingly well in her nineties, yet I find myself tightening with fear. Will my mom ultimately fare as well? I can only hope so. My mother and her friend are only about thirteen years apart. Eighty becomes ninety becomes a hundred.

Eightyninetyonehundreddeath. That's how my mind works.

Recently, my student Kate was sitting in my office, wanting to resume a conversation we had a couple semesters ago about her anxiety and depression, and this time she shared with me how she was worried about her mom. She said she inherited her anxiety and depression from her mother. And then, as I was inhaling my salad, she said to me, "I just can't imagine anything ever happening to my mom. I wouldn't be able to go on. I wouldn't be able to function." I understood what she was saying, of course, but found myself wanting to hold it at arm's length, not wanting to be drawn into more of that same fear. But there it was, because this sort of fear lives in the room. I had nothing to say to truly reassure her. I just listened and said, "Kate, I understand. More than you can imagine. But you have to remember, right now your mom is okay. That is not what's happening now. Try to be with what's happening now." Essentially, I was just talking to myself.

Every time my mother has a moment of ill health, even fairly run-of-the-mill issues, I wonder if this is foreshadowing something I don't yet know, like when my dad had his accident. I don't want her to lose all her faculties like my dad did. If she's around, I want, above all, for her to be able to talk to me. I imagine I will want her opinions more when she is dead than I even want them now, and I rely on them a lot now. She walks every day, and I've wondered if she will be killed crossing the street. She drives hours every week, commuting for her art classes and so she can use a printing press at a university that is more than an hour from her house each way. I worry that she will be killed in a car wreck, perhaps on one of the bridges between Cape Cod and wherever she is going. I don't want her taken from me suddenly. But when I weigh that possibility against what my dad went through, I have come to grips with the idea that if she dies doing something she loves, it could be okay, maybe even better. I worry about her being alive like my dad was at the end, with so little capacity, because I believe she has more to lose than my dad did. She has more things she is passionate about and more activities: she goes downstairs to the studio in her basement and makes art; she walks; she goes back and forth to her favorite little library in Cotuit and devours books; she studies the *New Yorker* magazine; she ventures out to all the newest, edgiest theaters, films, concerts, and exhibits; and she makes her own soups and bakes her own homemade bread, not in a bread machine, but all by hand. I can't imagine any one of these things being taken away from her, but most especially not her art. I remember teaching a course called Women in Society some years back, and I invited my mom to speak at the class to talk about women artists and the creative process. I will never forget when she told my students, "A life without my art would be very empty for me." I can't bear to think of her that hollowed out.

I have a million questions I know I should ask my mother—things I should ask now, while she is alive and still remembers everything, things I am sure I might want to know later, things I worry about not having the answer to. What was the best thing she ever did in her life? What does she regret? What's her advice for how best to live life?

What was the most important thing she learned from her mother? What was that funny story she used to tell about her friend Nanci? How did she make chocolate mousse pie? What does she think of this new type of apple? What was her favorite part about teaching? How did she actually get the troubled high school kid who couldn't spell his street name to suddenly write poetry? How did she come to teach like that, so fearlessly, so creatively? What's the secret to making homemade bread? What's her funniest memory of me as a kid? What should I do with the hundreds and hundreds of paintings and prints she made that are stored in her basement? Did she like Frida Kahlo? I can't remember. Where on earth is she most glad she traveled? Where does she wish she went? How did she really feel when she learned that her first husband had died long after they were divorced? What does she wish she could say now to my father, her second husband?

I remember being in the car with Mike after visiting with my mom at her house on the Cape. It was already a loaded trip. It was only my second time returning to New England after two years of living in South Carolina, and it was Mike's first time ever going there. Things had been tense between my mother and me as they often were in these infrequent but very long visits. We used to see each other often when I lived in Boston, and so less was riding on the time we spent together. We'd meet for lunch and take a long walk and maybe stroll into and out of a few boutiques or sit at a café and chat, and by early evening, we would each go back home, having not driven each other completely crazy.

Since I moved to South Carolina, we only see each other a few times a year, and our time together often becomes very intense. There is a lot of snapping at each other, lots of misfires, lots of me feeling like I am rendered twelve years old again. So when Mike and I got in the car to drive the ninety minutes back to the hotel, we were unusually quiet—not our typical, calm, relaxed quiet, but more of a tense, something-lingers-under-the-surface quiet. He remarked, "You really don't get along very well with your mom, do you?" And I burst into tears, unable to even speak. He found my crying unnerving. I found his comment unnerving. Right in that moment, my very deepest fears were realized. Of course, I couldn't really blame him; he was just stating what he had observed, and I was grateful that he was honest enough to say it. But I knew that what he saw was filtered through a prism of partial perspective, an incomplete picture I'd never be able to make whole for either of us. He never met my parents with me, all together, and he had only spent a few occasions with my mother. And he met me in the rawness of my grief, just a little more than three months after my dad died.

Essentially, in that moment in the car, Pencil Person was frantically jumping around in the backseat and then climbed into the front seat and sat between us, lodged right there, not moving. I was stunned and scared. His words also made me feel like we were a vulnerable, new couple. I felt the fragility that people often experience when they start dating someone new. But we had already been together a year and a half and seemed to possess a familiarity and intimacy that surpassed that time frame. That intimacy usually gave me total confidence in both our present and our future. And yet I wondered if Mike could and would still fully love me, understand me, and even want to be with me after witnessing this sort of family tension, seeing these other sides of me, with people close to me. And I worried that maybe he was right, that what he noticed was true—that getting along in person with my mom was often too hard and that maybe this somehow invalidated the connection I thought she and I shared. And what he said made me worried that she would die while we weren't getting along. Or worse, that he would leave me and she would die, or she would die and he would leave me. But either way, I worried I would be completely alone. And I felt exposed. I had not yet met Mike's siblings and their spouses and their children. I had only met his mother for a few hours, a quick stopover on our drive back from Asheville to Charleston. It was a simple enough meeting; she had drinks and snacks for us, he helped her fix some stuff on her computer, and we talked for a couple of hours and then headed home. So we had only met each other's mothers, but I knew that in my case, my mom was the only family I would have to show to him—ever—and apparently it already looked too dysfunctional. I had so longed to find a partner who understood the cast of characters, who got me in the context of my family, who would accept it all and not judge me. Sensing that what he had said was searing, Mike immediately wanted to take it back. Our trip had just begun, and we still had another week of vacation. Neither of us wanted it spoiled. Since then, when we have talked about that evening, he still apologizes for what he asked me, claiming it was a stupid thing to say. But it really wasn't, because it made me open up to him about my fears of losing my mom and my concern that he doesn't know enough of my family to know me as well as I want to be known. He tries to convince me otherwise.

Mike rarely talks about his father, and I usually worry about asking too many questions. I am incredibly curious about who he was mainly because I believe that we have more information about our partners when we know more about the people who raised them. And early on, Mike told me that his mom had said that he reminds her of her late husband, that they share a similar sense of humor. Obviously, his dad must have been funny as hell.

Days later on our trip, we went to Harvard Square for dinner. Over mashed potato pizza and beer, Mike told me that as a small child, he was supposed to accompany his father on a business trip. It was a special thing his dad had planned for all five kids, and they were scheduled to go in order of descending age. Mike is smack in the middle of his siblings. His oldest sister and brother got to go on these grown-up road trips, got to see their dad as a traveling salesman, got to stay in a hotel with him alone and have that coveted time with him all to themselves. But Mike's father collapsed in the bathroom and died suddenly of a heart attack, and Mike, his dad's next travel companion, was left without a trip, without a dad. Mike knows that when my family had trips planned, my dad often threatened not to go or threatened to leave and come home early. "We're not going" must sound so asinine to a man who was once a little boy who only knew "Sorry, but now you can't go."

I sat there listening to Mike, my eyes welling up with tears for this beautiful man I adore. The restaurant was pretty dark, and I am not sure Mike could see I was starting to cry. Plus, I wanted to conceal the tears. I had already cried twice on our vacation from all my worry, and I couldn't risk being seen a third time. I was starting to drive even myself crazy with my relentless worry.

Mike has never once expressed concern that the women in his life did not get to meet his dad. Gosh, *he* barely met his dad. He's almost fifty-nine now and has had nearly fifty years without his father. I've asked him if he remembers enough to have memories, to miss him, and understandably, he says that he missed getting to know him. Knowing Mike, I think it's his dad who's the one who really, truly missed out.

When you meet a partner later in life as Mike and I did, in our forties and fifties, there are huge chunks of life that just by necessity have fallen away, perhaps that we each wish we knew about the other but that in the end are no longer relevant. I find strange comfort in being with a man very much at home with his own incomplete, abbreviated narrative, so much more relaxed than I am in not letting that matter. He tries to show me how to do this nonworrying acceptance of death, with life being topsy-turvy and fragmented and impermanent, and ever so slowly, I learn how to live.

19

Change of Address

I've learned that forwarded mail goes on for years, even long after someone dies. It might be the one thing that has the potential to make even the insurmountable ravages of grief outrageously hilarious. I mean, really, who's that desperate to make money that they send promotional offers to dead people? Having my father's mail forwarded made me dread opening the mailbox. It made me sad beyond anything you can imagine, it taunted my memory and threatened to make me crazy, and it's one of the funniest things ever. Seriously.

The other night I was on the phone with my friend Tom, who lost his mother and father within fourteen months of each other, his father from congestive heart failure and his mother from early onset Alzheimer's. What happened to Tom's parents is sort of like what happened to my dad, whose death certificate indicates he died from congestive heart failure but who also suffered from dementia with agitation for years. The "with agitation" part always cracked me up, to be honest. It still does. For most of his life, he was cogent with agitation. Agitation was hardly a revealing or interesting part of the diagnosis.

Good friends since freshman year of college, Tom and I knew each other's families. His parents felt familiar to me and mine to him. While I have numerous friends who have lost a parent, especially those who tragically lost one in childhood, Tom is one of the only friends I have who had a parent in a nursing home for so long and who understands the particularly gross aspects of what that involves. Over the years, we have talked about what it meant to anticipate losing a parent, what it felt like to have a parent in a nursing home, and the work involved to help them die with dignity. Now we find ourselves talking about life after death—what we still have to do, what we are still confronted with, what we are still responsible for. At some point he and I started talking about how we still get mail for our dead parents; when they were alive, we had each arranged to have our parents' mail forwarded to us. It makes some practical sense when they are still alive to be able to get their mail and deal with any unpaid bills, answer any random letters, share with them who still thinks of them and sends a card. Like my father when he was well and living on his own, Tom's dad loved to be the first to get the mail, to sort through it, to read it. In some ways, it seemed wrong to get their mail, to open it. It was intercepting something we were not supposed to see.

I'm still getting seductive credit card offers for my dad though he died on Medicaid with a whopping $43.28 in his resident trust account at the nursing home. I joke with Mike that we should fill out the credit card applications and go on a big trip. There's the notice I received just last week labeled "Immediate Response Required" that requested that my dad update his vehicle service contract on his Toyota Avalon, a car we had returned years ago. There's the fine jewelry and antique silver store my dad went to with a girlfriend he wanted to impress and buy things for, and they still send him information about all their sales and events. As if he might one day go back and get her something. And then there are the advertisements for stair-climbing wheelchairs. I'm thankful we never had a need for those. In a "Well, I can top that" voice, Tom told me that he gets offers for hearing tests and hearing aids for his dead mother. And he still gets letters for his dead parents soliciting them for retirement planning and estate planning even long after he finalized what would be written on their graveside markers.

I asked Tom if he ever told his mother that his father had died. His mom, an avid exerciser, was always in amazing physical shape; it always appeared that she would outlive his father, maybe by decades. But once early onset Alzheimer's hit, it was reasonable to assume that she would go first. When his father wound up being the first one to die, Tom wasn't sure if he should tell his mother or not. Would she understand? What would she be able to process? In her rapidly shrinking, distorted brain, who was that man who died? Who was this man who was telling her the news? After all, Tom had become just a nice, nameless man who visited her.

As my father deteriorated in the nursing home, I kept feeling like we were in a continuous, cruel game of hide-and-seek. I found myself wanting to say to him, "Daddy, come out, come out wherever you are." But illnesses like dementia seem to make people retreat and spiral far inward, in ways where the core sense of who they are just gets harder and harder to access. It's absolutely maddening.

"Isn't it the craziest thing to have to tell one parent that the other died?" I asked Tom. I didn't have to ask. I know it is. I had to do this too. Sitting cross-legged by myself on the floor of the airport in Savannah, Georgia, I called my mom on Cape Cod to tell her that my dad had just died in Cleveland—a man she had once loved, whom she had once married. It was as though you could draw a line on a map of how the news traveled from Ohio to Georgia and then to Massachusetts and then back to Ohio, and you would have a triangle shape. My mom always said that she hated the number three and how our family dynamic became two against one, and here on the day my dad died was this surreal, painful, triangular geography staring right in my face. I think I always imagined that the three of us would be together when something dreadful like this happened or that my mother would call me from his bedside in Cleveland to tell me that he died.

On the night of my wedding to Mark, watching me all grown up and getting married, my father, in his toast to us, asked sweetly, nostalgically, with a break in his voice, "Where is the little girl I carried?" I understand now what he must have been longing for. I long for it too—a time when the family roles were firmly in place, not reversed and uncomfortable. Tom told me how he feels like he has to be "the new patriarch" now for his son. For any legacy of sons who will come forward. Dealing with our ill parents forces us to assume new roles. How we deal with their deaths then requires a whole new change of address, not just for the mail we get for them but also, and maybe most importantly, in how we come to address ourselves.

We inhabit a space with our dying parents, this space that forces us to change directions all the time, accompany them on detours and wrong turns, and deal with changed and canceled plans. It's more than a space—it's much more all-consuming than that. It's like its own home that we have to live in, at least for a while, usually years. A home built of grief. But it's a home we have no blueprints for, no sense of how to construct it, no sense of where the exits are or how to ultimately have it razed. Like termites that burrow into a house's very foundation, grief gets in and gnaws away. Deaths never stop. They just change direction. They change form.

And then, I believe—well, I believe because I hope—there may come a time where we realize we can't live there anymore, not like that. Where the heavy emptiness of that dwelling is just too much to bear. Where we can come to declare, if only to ourselves, "I don't live here anymore." It will be its own special sort of change of address.

Epilogue

If you got to this place in the book, thank you. It means that you withstood a story of brokenness—and wholeness—told in fragments. If I succeeded at all as a writer, I took you on a journey that led you to understand that in this story, there was, and remains, no pure protagonist or antagonist. When you first heard me say that my father was abusive, you might have assumed you could or would hate him. Or you might be like a few people with whom I attended a writing workshop a few years ago who commented about how much they loved my dad. If you found yourself loving him, or liking him, or finding him complicated and troubled yet strangely endearing, you get it. In fact, you might better understand how it's so common to want and to desperately need bad, mean, abusive behavior to stop while still wanting and needing the relationship with the person to continue. You understand that it's possible to love intensely and to fear just often enough to then question the love and that when the love is bone deep, you start to question if you still had the right to be so afraid. Relationships, lives, selves are all blended. Everything is always blended.

Before I could access the depth, vibrancy, and richness I enjoy in my life now, and especially that I'm lucky enough to share with Mike, I did have to endure loss. In my yoga class last week, the teacher reminded us that those who have trembled the most are the strongest. My dad's years of illness and decline, and ultimately his death, opened me to a depth of pain I had never before encountered, but it also opened my worried heart further still.

Almost fifteen years have passed since my dad fell and his life as he and I knew it came crashing down with him; for nearly half that time, he has been gone, a little more than seven years. What I see now is that his death opened me and made me more compassionate and vulnerable toward myself. The Buddhist meditation teacher Sharon Salzberg says, "Compassion is a state of mind that is itself open, abundant, and inclusive; it allows us to meet pain more directly."

The thing about being open, compassionate, and vulnerable with ourselves about our pain is that we can then, hopefully, extend this to others, to hold open and compassionate space for others' vulnerability and pain. Healing from abuse almost always means bearing witness to it in front of others and accessing a voice of resistance. The weight of caregiving carries with it a similar texture of hypervigilance, of being on guard, of never knowing what might happen next, of doing everything to safeguard against another impending disaster, and caregiving is all about bearing witness. For me, caregiving wasn't so much about finding voice but about wanting to scream most of the time. And every time I tried, and every time I did, the experience of caregiving nudged me toward a tender curiosity, toward my dad and back on myself. It turns out that writing does all of this also. It demands that we pay close attention and invite all the tenderness and curiosity possible to cultivate voice.

Just as the best part of someone's personality can also have a shadow side and be their worst quality, the beauty of memoir is also its curse. The exquisite quality of memoir is how it is a slice of life, deeply exposed, coupled with the understanding that life is dynamic and emergent and that the characters you might have gotten attached to have changed, maybe in ways that deepen and extend the story or possibly in ways that contradict it or at least alter it. While working on this book, I had a conversation with my editor in which she described how reading memoirs can be like picking up jewels; looking at them intently; and inspecting their shapes, facets, and colors, and then you begin to feel curious how they all hang together. I think that's true. And I also think something else happens, and this is the curse of memoir—or at least what troubles the water of memoir. Time passes, people die, friendships change, the writer's perception shifts again. Nothing is fixed. It's never fixed. It's always blended.

And if you're like me as a reader, you long to know what is now happening with the writer. At least at the last moment in time she can possibly tell you. And you might hope and expect that the journey you endured with her changed and bettered her and made her whole and maybe even set her up to ride the next grief waves with more grace. It's true that I do feel somewhat less anxious and somewhat more accepting and comfortable around grief than I used to be. But that's not saying very much, since I had so damn far to go.

I'd like to be able to say that I'm also less anxious and more accepting and comfortable around anticipatory grief and loss, but it wouldn't be true. I'm not that evolved yet. I'm still nervous when I think of losing the people I love. I'm afraid—and very exhausted by being this afraid—of potentially, eventually, maybe even probably walking the world without family. Because, remember, I don't have siblings. Therefore, I don't have nieces and nephews. My parents' strained and estranged relationships with their own relatives did not leave me in a position to be close to extended family. I don't have children, and so I won't have grandchildren, and now, my mother is not the same as when I wrote earlier chapters of this book. And Mike is insistent that at the end, I will be the one wiping his ass, kissing him goodbye, and then running off with a new man, sailing around the world or some other wild scenario. My fantasy is that he'll live forever.

So let me get back to the reality of where we all are now, or at least where we seem to be for the moment. As I finish this book and send it off into the world, I have lost my mother. However, my mom is not dead yet. Her worst qualities have become her only qualities. Her best disappeared. In the chapter "The Worry Machine," I worried about my mom being hit in traffic while taking her walks or driving to and from an art studio. I was worried about how life would hit her, arrest her, and kill her. I was not prepared for nearly the same thing happening to my mother as what happened to my father—that she would have a heart attack, then later fall at the grocery store and have a brain bleed, and then five months after that fall in the bathroom while holding a glass bowl, which left her sitting on shards of glass strewn around on cold tile, alone at 4:30 a.m.

In the chapter "Medical Records," where I thought about how we are told of the deaths of people closest to us, I anticipated that my mom's partner, Allan, would call me to tell me if anything happened to my mom. That will no longer happen, as he has been moved to a memory care center, where he packs his laundry basket thinking it's a suitcase so his parents can pick him up from his college dorm and wanders into another woman's room down the hall who undresses in front of him. One day when my mom went to visit Allan in the nursing home, another resident declared, "Sacramento is the capital of dementia."

When my father got sick, I was the first of most of my friends to deal with caregiving and the loss of a parent. Now I am one of the first to face losing both parents. Much like when my dad first got sick, I feel like I can't catch up, like I'm running after my mother as she slips away. When a parent makes this turn, it's a breathless feeling.

I still need to ask my mom where she got that yellow stew pot I should use and still never have. I should have asked more about that principal named Boyd she loved when she taught school, who was a great mentor for her. I can't remember if she likes Chekov's writing or not. And she needs to tell me what she really wants me to do with the hundreds and hundreds of paintings and prints she has made over the years that are in her basement studio or what she really loved most about me. And when my dear friend Helene tells me that for her daughters' sixteenth birthdays, she bought them vibrators so they would know how to please themselves and develop a healthy sexuality, I realize that in all my mom's eccentricity and being ahead of her time, whole chunks of life fell off the list of what we talked about—like sexuality, orgasms, and more about her girlhood and emerging womanhood. Sometimes I make a list of things to ask her, but the conversations are abbreviated; she's too depressed, withdrawn, and reclusive to talk much. And she has always been exceedingly private. She insists I not come visit her. She doesn't want to see anyone other than the women coming to her house for around-the-clock care. No one in my life seems to understand why I have not gone there, even to surprise her. But she hates surprises, always has.

One of the hardest things about my dad when he was well—and when he was not—was that I had too much of him. But really the opposite is true of my mother. I realize I do not truly know my mom in all the ways I wanted, or needed, or hoped for. Parents shield kids from certain things, and by the time an adult child finds the parent unusually fascinating and fully separate, the parent's walls are up and solid, and then their health deteriorates. For my whole life, my mother has told me that life is a solo flight, that we are born alone and die alone, and that maybe, if we are lucky enough, we have a few people in between who are on our side. But I think that sensibility comes from a fear of abandonment. If she pushes others away first, she can't feel left behind. If she refuses to see people and dies alone, she can be right, that we really are all alone. And for her, being right is supremely important.

Defiantly and fiercely, I have tried like hell to prove her wrong, to craft a life of enduring connection and fictive kin, with enough solitude to give me spaciousness and renewal but with buoys to safeguard against the extreme loneliness she promised would be inevitable. I want so badly for the narrative of my life and the end of my story to be different than my parents'. I don't know how any of this will turn out or where and how I will be, but I can try and I can hope.

We never know when a beginning is a beginning and when an ending is an ending. For example, what was scheduled to be a brief first date for lunch with Mike lasted eleven hours, though driving to meet him late that morning, I definitely had no idea what we were beginning. In the same way, when Mike and I went to visit my mom last June, I had no way of knowing, however much I was paying attention to what was her noticeable slippage, that our dinner out at a nice nearby restaurant would become one of her last times out of the house or that when she took us to the beach, it would be one of her last times driving and seeing the ocean.

Each new beginning, each new ending, calls out to us to pay attention, to make new memories.

Many years ago, my mom told me a story about a time she went to see her mother in a nursing home and a resident there greeted her and said, "Welcome to wherever we are." It struck me as one of the most depressing, empty, and odd things I had ever heard. Healing from the grief of abuse and from the grief of caregiving and loss helped me see that dark comment in new ways—as surprisingly accurate and with open hope for what is.

Wherever we are is where I met you. Wherever we are is also where I leave you.

Acknowledgments

Like many writers, I have dreamed of the moment that publication would be so imminent that it would be time to write my acknowledgments. And now it is here, and words are suddenly failing me. I am coming up short when trying to describe the meaning and impact of certain people in my life. And there's a whole universe of people for whom I am grateful.

I credit Mary Gilfus for being the first intellectual in my life to give me the language to name and the tools to question and understand dynamics of domestic violence. Entering both of her classes at the University of Wisconsin–Madison, I had no idea the path she was putting me on nor the extent to which I would benefit and heal from turning the central questions in the field back onto my own life. For the ways she turned on my feminist imagination, my life has forever benefitted, and for her enduring lifelong friendship all these years later, I am even more grateful still.

It was in class with Mary that I first learned about Emerge, the groundbreaking abuser intervention program located in Boston, and I intuited that one day, that would be compelling work for me. Later, I was delighted to have the honor of working there alongside fearless, tireless advocates for social change who taught and inspired me beyond belief. I also recall many of the abusers with whom I worked for helping me to rethink assumptions about intimacy and violence. I am blessed to have had the opportunity to meet and work with giants in the field of domestic violence intervention—namely, David Adams and Susan Cayouette. I am so lucky to have learned from their ideas that have helped shape the worldwide movement to end intimate partner violence. I am thankful for the conversations years ago with Susan Clare and Shirley and Larry Bostrom that helped me rethink issues of motives, mind-set, forgiveness, healing, and redemption.

My thinking about the issues that figure prominently in this book has benefited greatly from comments and questions from former and current students, colleagues at academic conferences, and audience members at community events when I have given talks. Many of these people whom I don't know pushed me to wrestle more with my own ideas.

I wish to thank Stephen Mansfield, who chose to publish my very first piece of creative nonfiction. He was the guest editor for "Writing the Father," a special issue of the journal *Life Writing* that first published "Sugar," which appears in this book. Soon after that, I responded to a call for book chapters put out by Catherine (Kay) Valentine and Donna King for their collection *Letting Go*; I am grateful to them for selecting "The Gold Pen" to be part of their anthology and to *Utne Reader* for choosing to reprint it. It was the receptivity to those two essays that sparked my intention to write this book.

I am grateful to my agent, George Greenfield of CreativeWell Inc., who recognized my tenacity and took a chance to represent me and whose name is absolutely synonymous with *mensch*; I look forward to more creative collaborations with him. Every first-time author should be lucky enough to have an editor like Kimberly Guinta. Immediately receptive to the book proposal, Kim propelled the project along and kept me confident that Rutgers

University Press would be a fabulous place from which to launch this book into the world. I appreciate the entire team at Rutgers for thoughtful and careful consideration of my work. Courtney Brach and Jeremy Grainger have been especially kind, supportive, and creative. I appreciate Alissa Zarro's support with the final production of this book. Special thanks to Stephanie Grimm for her availability and interest in supporting my project so it would be ready for production. And I appreciate all that Scribe Inc. did to make this book happen, particularly Daniel Constantino, copyeditor extraordinaire, and Megan Grande.

I have been studying memoir in earnest since 2003 and have benefited from writing workshops I have taken, especially with Sue William Silverman, Rebecca McClanahan, Ariel Levy, Andre Dubus III, and Joan Wickersham. GrubStreet in Boston and the Fine Arts Work Center in Provincetown, Massachusetts, provided me with opportunities to participate in workshops and to find supportive communities of writers with whom I have developed important connections and friendships. I recognize here, too, a web of creative mentors whom I may never meet but whose music, poetry, dance, art, and writing grace my life and blast energy into me and my work—and especially Rosanne Cash, who seems to know a lot about complicated, creative fathers and whose album *The River and the Thread* was on repeat as I wrote the bulk of this book.

A formative part of accessing my creativity and the art of letting go took place with Abby Seixas and her innovative, powerful, and therapeutic Deep River Groups for women. Her groups, designed to help women like myself transcend the deadening minutiae of list making and crazy making and access the deeper flow of passion, creativity, and possibility, changed me in profound ways. The women in the groups—the women of the deep river—became for me like anchors on the shores of discovery, depth, and passion.

I am beyond grateful to every friend mentioned in stories throughout the book as well as to other very important friends whose names did not land on these pages but who have made an indelible mark on my life. Last names have only been mentioned when I had permission to do so. In almost every case, all first names that appear throughout the book are real names; I assigned pseudonyms to certain people and places mentioned to protect confidentiality. Similarly, all students' names have been changed to protect privacy.

My very special thanks go to my former colleague, dear friend, and big sister extraordinaire Pat John, to whom I literally feel I owe my life as it is currently configured. Our friendship originated in grief and has been saturated with love ever since. I am thankful to her son, Jason, whom I was never lucky enough to meet but whose memory is inscribed on a bumper sticker on her car, which prompted me to ask about him. And it was that little sticker that formed the basis of a truly neverending conversation that started at the curbside parking for airport drop-offs. It is only because of Pat's encouragement that I considered the move to South Carolina in 2012 for my current job and that I was then in a position to find the love of my life in Mike Robertson, a man who completely jumpstarted my writing. So I am grateful to Pat for helping me find home—at the university, in the Lowcountry, with Mike, and in my writing.

Side by side with my dearest childhood friends Erica, Renee, and Betsy, I learned to read and write in elementary school; I only dreamed that those skills would lead to doing work like this. I am glad I have these lifelong sisterfriends who remember the beginnings and, by doing so, embody hope and remind me of all the amazing directions and turns my life can still take. When I have spoken to them about this book, they have radiated nothing but excitement and pride, and for all this and so much more, I feel very lucky.

I thank Livia Pohlman Hartgrove for being my other best big sister in the whole wide world, for exuding beauty and bravery always, for stretching me to rethink creativity and courage, for always thinking I have interesting things to say, and for being, for me, one of the most amazing people in the entire world to talk to. She has been a key person in reminding me for many, many years to find and preserve the time to cultivate a creative life and to write my heart and guts out, always and regardless of anything else.

I'm grateful to Janine Schipper for being the sort of friend where the deepest connection is felt regardless of time and space—and for living on a higher spiritual plane than pretty much anyone I know and from which I have learned a great deal. Her gifts of radical, soulful self-acceptance buoy me as I continue to clarify what I value most in my career and my life.

My loving gratitude goes to these special friends who are really more like family: Nancy Coppelman, Mary-Jane Eisen, Julie Fohrman, Jen Nash, and Helene Suh (a.k.a. my Crazy Zen Sister). Their life experiences and expertise on things like aging, dementia, caregiving, only children, mental health, healing, and self-care have made all the difference. They have each helped me tackle big life questions while simultaneously considering how best to accompany someone else at the end of life and be a friend to ourselves in the process and how to artfully craft a juicy, zestful, and meaningful life. And the best part is the fun and laughter I share with each of them.

I am grateful to Emily Kane, a former professor of mine, a lifelong mentor, and a woman who over the years has become more friend and family to me than anything else. She has lovingly cheered me on as I have pursued public, creative sociology. She's able to pierce the center of big issues, opening them up so I want to endlessly explore every facet with her.

For half of my life, I have benefitted from my rich, treasured friendship with C. J. Churchill. His perspective on anything and everything challenges and sharpens my thinking. Writers often struggle with when they can call themselves writers, and C. J. has helped me articulate, both inwardly and outwardly, the unfolding context of my career as a writer. His loving friendship is easily one of the greatest gifts of my life.

I owe a special debt to my friend and ex-husband Mark for understanding how important it has been for me to write this book into being. Thank you, Mark, for the love and care you showed my father and that you still show me.

I am forever grateful to my mother for cultivating in me early on an interest in both how to observe and how to make art. I thank her for her poetic, artistic, and unconventional ways, for helping me think in image and metaphor and for quite possibly being the first person in helping me learn how to look and pay attention. That quality, nurtured in me in art museums throughout the world, may have been the first and most important writing tool I ever really needed.

I recall my father scouring my prose for me when I was a kid writing papers for school; the process was agonizing as I recall, though if I write well at all, I credit most, if not all, of it to him. At the time, neither of us could have known I would take the story of our relationship and write, rewrite, and scour it alone with his spirit by my side. I have come to see that through writing, we come to learn what we know, and through it, we think and grow. I am eternally grateful to my father for helping me hone and value this life skill that often frustrates me but more often than not sustains and nourishes me. I feel both his presence and my loss every single day of my life.

After my first date with Mike, he asked if I would be willing to let him see any of my writing. I sent him "Sugar," and his response was beyond anything I could have hoped for. After only one date, he said he could imagine sitting with me at home or at a coffeehouse, eager to read and comment on drafts as I worked on the next piece. It conjured up a dreamy scene—warm coffee, an even hotter man, and cozying up with reading and writing and talking and tweaking stories. What started as an outstretched vision soon became my lived reality, and for that, I couldn't be happier. Michael—you are the single greatest source of joy in my entire life, and loving you is by far the easiest and most important thing I have ever gotten to do.

About the Author

DEBORAH J. COHAN is an associate professor of sociology at the University of South Carolina Beaufort. Her research and teaching interests include gender-based violence, issues of the body and sexuality, race, creative nonfiction, and education. Her work has appeared in numerous academic and nonacademic publications. Cohan is the author of the popular blog "Social Lights" for *Psychology Today*, she is a regular contributor to *Inside Higher Ed*, and she is often quoted in major media outlets. She earned a BA in sociology and a certificate in women's studies at the University of Wisconsin–Madison, an MA in sociology at the University of Texas at Austin, a joint MA in sociology and women's studies and a PhD in sociology from Brandeis University. Cohan lives in the Lowcountry of South Carolina. Learn more about her at deborahjcohan.com.